*C*ASES

IN

*L*ABOR

*R*ELATIONS

PRENTICE-HALL INDUSTRIAL RELATIONS AND PERSONNEL SERIES

DALE YODER, *Editor*

BELCHER—*Wage and Salary Administration, 2nd ed.*
BELLOWS—*Psychology of Personnel in Business and Industry, 3rd ed.*
BELLOWS, GILSON, AND ODIORNE—*Executive Skills*
BRINKER—*Social Security*
DAVEY—*Contemporary Collective Bargaining, 2nd ed.*
DUBIN—*Human Relations in Administration, 2nd ed.*
DUBIN—*Working Union-Management Relations*
ECKER, MACRAE, OUELLETTE, AND TELFORD—*Handbook for Supervisors*
GOMBERG—*A Trade Union Analysis of Time Study, 2nd ed.*
HEALY, HENDERSON, HINTZ, JARRETT, MARBUT, WHITE — *Creative Collective Bargaining: Meeting Today's Challenges to Labor-Management Relations*
MAHONEY—*Building the Executive Team*
MALICK AND VAN NESS—*Administrative Behavior*
OTIS AND LEUKERT—*Job Evaluation, 2nd ed.*
PFIFFNER AND FELS—*The Supervision of Personnel, 3rd ed.*
SHARTLE—*Executive Performance and Leadership*
SHARTLE—*Occupational Information, 3rd ed.*
SHOSTAK AND GOMBERG—*Blue-Collar World*
STONE AND KENDALL—*Effective Personnel Selection Procedures*
THOMPSON—*Personnel Management for Supervisors, 2nd ed.*
TOLLES—*Origins of Modern Wage Theories*
VOLLMER AND MILLS—*Professionalization*
YODER—*Personnel Management and Industrial Relations, 5th ed.*
YODER—*Personnel Principles and Policies, 2nd ed.*

CASES

IN

LABOR

RELATIONS

AN ARBITRATION EXPERIENCE

JOHN R. ABERSOLD

WAYNE E. HOWARD

Wharton School of Finance and Commerce
University of Pennsylvania

PRENTICE-HALL, INC., ENGLEWOOD CLIFFS, NEW JERSEY

Library of Congress Catalog Card No.: 67-12602

PRENTICE-HALL INTERNATIONAL, INC., *London*
PRENTICE-HALL OF AUSTRALIA, PTY. LTD., *Sidney*
PRENTICE-HALL OF CANADA, LTD., *Toronto*
PRENTICE-HALL OF INDIA (PRIVATE) LTD., *New Delhi*
PRENTICE-HALL OF JAPAN, INC., *Tokyo*

Current Printing (last digit):
10   9   8   7   6   5   4   3   2

PRINTED IN THE UNITED STATES OF AMERICA
C-11879

Preface

Since the arbitration of labor disputes is a relatively small part of the industrial relations function, the question might well be raised as to why cases in arbitration are used to illustrate problem areas in industrial relations. Two basic answers are suggested. First, arbitration issues focus attention on the presumably more difficult problems arising in labor-management relations, since these problems are ones which the parties have been unable or unwilling to resolve. Though the ambiguities of contract language or the lack of good relations between the parties may contribute to the volume of cases arbitrated, it is a fair presumption that many arbitrations develop because of the difficulties in resolving the underlying conflicts in social or economic philosophy expressed in these issues. Second, the arbitration process as an orderly procedure for determining the facts and the conflicting positions of management and labor in their interpretation of those facts permits one to encapsulate a broad history of labor relations in a relatively condensed digest of the problem, something which cannot be achieved with realistic case studies of negotiation sessions or grievance meetings.

A final reason explaining the format of this casebook is simply that the writers are labor arbitrators as well as teachers and have naturally attempted to put their experience to use within the classroom. The original work which gave impetus to this volume was an attempt to formulate relatively short and realistic case studies for implementing the textual material in an advanced undergraduate course in collective bargaining. These case studies are not so much regarded as problems in quasi-legal decision making as illustrations of the insight needed to understand the human and institutional problems of collective bargaining.

The writers have drawn upon their experience in arbitration to compile a series of arbitration cases, which in their opinion, represent the common areas of employer-employee differences with respect to the meaning and application of contract terminology. While the factual material and the opposing arguments of the parties have been considerably condensed, each of these cases has been presented in arbitration before the writers in essentially the same manner as presented herein; neither the facts nor the arguments have been altered. Identities of companies and individuals have, of course, been hidden.

The following areas have been selected:

1. Arbitrability of grievances
2. Discipline
3. Wages
4. Vacations and holidays
5. Work assignment
6. Seniority
7. Distribution of overtime
8. Subcontracting
9. Impact of technological change.

These areas have been selected not only on the basis of the frequency of disputes occurring within a given area, but also on the basis of the variety of human relations and institutional problems in industrial relations which are revealed in attempts at the resolution of disputes in these areas.

Each subject is introduced by means of a brief summary of the problems and issues encountered in the application of collective bargaining agreements in that particular area. These summaries are intended to raise questions rather than to settle issues. From three to six case studies dealing with different aspects of the subject under discussion are then presented. Each case study has appended appropriate discussion questions. Finally, a selected bibliography accompanies each problem area to aid in more detailed study of the problems which have been presented.

After careful consideration the writers decided not to include any summary of the decisions arrived at by the arbitrators. In the first place, all these cases were decided by one or the other of the writers. Presumably other arbitrators may well have decided certain of them differently, or based their decision on a different logical framework.

It is not the intention of the writers to impose on the reader their views of how specific issues should be approached.

More important, the writers felt that inclusion of the decision would substantially reduce the usefulness of these cases as a teaching medium by focusing upon the arbitral solution, which may not be the best solution to the problem underlying the issue. As the cases stand, they can be used in personnel courses by focusing on the wisdom of management action rather than on the propriety of such action. They can be used in human relations courses by stressing the human and institutional conflicts underlying the specific dispute. They are also useful in industrial relations courses to indicate how parties may avoid some of these problems through more careful negotiation or how they may avoid the arbitration of the problems through more effective work in the early steps of the grievance procedure. At the same time these cases can be used by students of labor law or arbitration by concentrating on that aspect of the cases.

The writers are grateful for the assistance of Mrs. Helen S. White in the preparation of the manuscript, and wish to express their appreciation for the patience and co-operation of their wives, Catherine S. Abersold and Jean W. Howard, while this work was in progress.

JOHN R. ABERSOLD

WAYNE E. HOWARD

Contents

1 INTRODUCTION, 1

2 ARBITRABILITY, 7

Text Summary, 7- 9

CASES
1. *The Jason Corporation Case, 10*
2. *The Larson Company Case, 14*
3. *The Kokomo Company Case, 19*

BIBLIOGRAPHY

3 DISCIPLINE, 24

Text Summary, 24-25

CASES
4. *The Foster Motor Freight Company Case, 26*
5. *The Cordon Manufacturing Company Case, 29*
6. *The De Forest Corporation Case, 33*
7. *The Appleton Company Case, 38*
8. *The Cole Company Case, 42*

BIBLIOGRAPHY

4 WAGES, 47

    Text Summary, 47-49

    CASES
        9. *The Waterville Company Case, 50*
      10. *The Ulster Company Case, 54*
      11. *The Victoria Company Case, 58*
      12. *The Tatem Company Case, 62*
      13. *The Sweetwater Company Case, 66*

    BIBLIOGRAPHY

5 VACATIONS AND HOLIDAYS

    Text Summary, 71-73

    CASES
      14. *The Newmark Company Case, 74*
      15. *The Oregon Company Case, 77*
      16. *The Maxwell Corporation Case, 81*
      17. *The Rangeley Company Case, 82*
      18. *The Bangor Company Case, 86*

    BIBLIOGRAPHY

6 WORK ASSIGNMENTS

    Text Summary, 91-93

    CASES
      19. *The Atlanta Aviation Company Case, 94*
      20. *The Armbruster Company Case, 99*
      21. *The Auburn Company Case, 105*
      22. *The Rumford Company Case, 108*
      23. *The Lewiston Company Case, 112*

    BIBLIOGRAPHY

7 SENIORITY, 118

Text Summary, 118-120

CASES
24. *The Applied Products Company Case, 121*
25. *The Babylonian Company Case, 126*
26. *The Cyclonic Corporation Case, 130*
27. *The Diamond Speciality Company Case, 133*
28. *The Excelsior Corporation Case, 137*
29. *The Quinlan Company Case, 141*

BIBLIOGRAPHY

8 DISTRIBUTION OF OVERTIME

Text Summary, 146-147

CASES
30. *The Bonita Company Case, 148*
31. *The Waterloo Corporation Case, 150*
32. *The Zenger Company Case, 154*
33. *The Young Company Case, 157*
34. *The Xavier Company Case, 160*
35. *The Collingswood Company Case, 164*

BIBLIOGRAPHY

9 SUBCONTRACTING

Text Summary, 168-169

CASES
36. *The Pennsylvania Company Case, 170*
37. *The Quaker Company Case, 173*
38. *The Roger Company Case, 178*

BIBLIOGRAPHY

10 THE IMPACT OF TECHNOLOGICAL CHANGE

   Text Summary, 183-185

   CASES
      39. The Linden Company Case, 186
      40. The Fletcher Company Case, 192
      41. The Haddon Chemical Company Case, 198
      42. The Hammonton Company Case, 206
      43. The Berlin Company Case, 212

   BIBLIOGRAPHY

CASES

IN

LABOR

RELATIONS

CHAPTER 1

Introduction

Disputes over the terms and conditions of employment are inherent in the employer-employee relationship. Such disputes have existed from the day when an employer hired his first employee. With the passage of time the nature of these disputes has changed, and, more importantly, a major alteration has occurred in the means of their resolution.

Before the advent of unionism, the means to resolve disputes were indirect and relatively ineffective. The employer unilaterally determined the conditions of employment; the employee could voice his dissatisfaction by quitting his job, or less blatantly, perhaps, by withholding a full measure of effort in the performance of his job. With the development of unions, an additional alternative was opened to the employee: he, and his fellow employees, could join together and react to management determination of employment conditions by a mass withholding of their services, a more direct and effective process for resolving these disputes.

When in 1935, with the passage of the Wagner Act, the national labor policy of the country became that of favoring the collective bargaining of wages and conditions of employment, the stage was set for the development of more effective and more efficient machinery for the resolution of these disputes. Under collective bargaining, representatives of the parties at interest, employers and employees, jointly agreed upon certain specified conditions of employment and incorporated them in a collective bargaining contract.

With few exceptions, disputes over the *negotiation* of collective bargaining agreements are *not resolved* through the arbitration process. Indeed, most employees, most unions, and most arbitrators are in substantial agreement that disputes over new contract terms do not lend themselves to this means of resolution. The vast majority of students of industrial relations practice believe that the parties, to the maximum extent possible, should be free to determine the conditions under which they offer and accept employment. Thus, third-party intervention in disputes over contract negotiation has rarely exceeded that of conciliation or mediation efforts when the parties are unable to agree. Rare exceptions do occur, in the public utility field in particular.

The mere fact that a labor agreement has been consumated, however, and that the conditions of employment have been set down and presumably stabilized over the life of such agreement does not mean that disputes will not arise over the meaning and application of its terms. What is "just cause" for discharge under an agreement in which the employer agrees to discharge employees "only upon a showing of just cause"? What is meant by "ability" when an employer agrees to promote employees in accordance with "seniority and ability"? The frank recognition that the parties are not so omniscient as to be able to set down in a collective agreement the sum total of these ground rules, but rather that the collective agreement becomes reformed and refined in the day-to-day relationships of the parties as evidenced in their practices and dispute settlements has become known as the *living document* theory of the labor contract. Provision for the settlement of disputes over the interpretation of agreement terms and their application to specific situations are normally made by the parties, themselves, through the establishment of grievance procedures in the labor agreement.

Where the parties have been unable to resolve a dispute, most agreements provide for the submission of the dispute to a third-party arbitrator who makes a final and binding determination of the issue. This so-called grievance arbitration has provided an orderly means for the resolution of disputes over the interpretation and application of the terms of a labor agreement. Arbitration provisions have thus become accepted as a *quid pro quo* for the union's agreement not to strike during the life of the labor contract.

THE ARBITRATION PROCESS

Technically speaking the arbitration process is carried out by carefully drawn collective bargaining provisions which define the jurisdiction and authority of the arbitrator, which stipulate the procedure for selecting an arbitrator and defraying the expenses of arbitration, and which express the parties' agreement to accept the award of the arbitrator as a final and binding settlement of the dispute. Questions over the jurisdiction and authority of the arbitrator can be quite complex and are treated separately in Chapter Two.

The parties may decide to use the permanent or impartial umpire type of arbitration, or in the alternative, to use the so-called *ad hoc* procedure of selecting a different arbitrator for each case or series of cases. Each of these methods offers certain advantages over the other, and the fact that both systems are widely used in the United States indicates that neither system is markedly superior under all circumstances. Some parties attempt to secure some of the advantages of each system by naming a specific panel of arbitrators in their agreement, from which panel they select a specific arbitrator for each pending case.

Some parties prefer the arbitration to be conducted by a single arbitrator; others prefer a board of arbitrators, most commonly composed of three arbitrators, a union arbitrator, a company arbitrator, and an impartial chairman. In practice such a board differs only slightly from the sole arbitrator proceeding since the union and company members are normally advocates for their respective parties rather than impartial third-party participants. While arbitration boards offer several distinct advantages to the arbitration process, they also can create pitfalls, particularly in those circumstances where the collective bargaining agreement requires that a majority decision of the board is necessary for a binding determination of the issue.

Frequently arbitrators are selected privately by the parties; in most cases permanent arbitrators or impartial umpires are selected in this fashion. In the vast majority of instances, however, selection is made from panels of arbitrators supplied to the parties by the American Arbitration Association, a private nonprofit organization, or by the Federal Mediation and Conciliation Service. A number of industrial states also maintain arbitration panels which are available to parties requesting them.

The arbitration proceedings in most instances are characterized by their informality. In most cases these are conducted in a conference table setting, and the relationship of the parties may range from formal to earthy. Attorneys may represent the parties but in many cases do not do so, and in a large number of cases one party may be so represented whereas the other is not. A transcript of the hearing may be taken, but in the majority of cases the only record of the proceeding is the arbitrator's handwritten notes. The arbitrator is not bound by the legal rules of evidence unless expressly required by the collective bargaining agreement establishing his jurisdiction and authority, and to the legalist, the handling of evidence may seem quite cavalier, unless the special function of the arbitrator is thoroughly appreciated. Normally, however, an orderly procedure is established whereby each party in turn presents its opening statement, its presentation of evidence including testimony of witnesses who are subject to the other party's cross-examination, and its final summarization reviewing its evidence and arguments. On occasion prehearing briefs are presented in lieu of opening statements, and frequently posthearing briefs are substituted for final summations. Usually the arbitrator has thirty days after the closing of the hearing or the receipt of posthearing briefs to render an award accompanied by a written opinion setting forth the reasons for his decision.

FUNCTION OF THE ARBITRATOR

The arbitration process is quasi-judicial in nature, and the arbitrator is most commonly described as a private judge responsible only to the parties who select him. Similar in some respects to those of the public judiciary, the functions of the arbitrator can be more clearly delineated by contrasting them with those of the judge, rather than by listing their common similarities.

In certain respects the arbitrator has broader powers of decision-making than his public counterpart. Unlike the judge, he is not bound by the precedent of other arbitrators; the principle of *stare decisis* does not apply in labor arbitration. While courts will enforce his award on the petition of either party, his decisions are not in the truest sense appealable to the courts, since in most jurisdictions arbitration awards are appealable only on narrow grounds, none of which is directly related to the soundness or correctness of his decision.

The arbitrator is more of a specialist than the typical judge whose decision-making may well cover the whole gamut of human conflict. Indeed, it is his expertise in what has been termed "the common law of the shop" that has resulted in the voluntary delegation of broad decision-making power to the arbitrator. For unlike other litigants the parties to a collective bargaining agreement cannot escape each other. The decisions of the arbitrator must not only meet the theoretical tests of logic, but the pragmatic test of whether they will work out in the future day-to-day relationships in the plant. Moreover, he must have some understanding of the institutional needs of the parties which may cause them to agree in negotiations, yet frame their agreement in deliberately ambiguous language, or deliberately engage thereafter in completely contrary practices. The agreement may express or hide the true intent of the parties to it, and can be interpreted only by one who has come to understand these nuances. What is needed is judicious rather than judicial interpretation.

This does not mean that the arbitrator has an unlimited scope of authority, nor that he decides issues on the basis of subjective reaction. Quite to the contrary, he is still the interpreter of the total agreement between the parties, composed as it may be of negotiative intent, express language, and the body of practice which has developed under the collective bargaining relationship. The function of creating the framework of principles belongs to the parties in the negotiating process; the arbitrator's function is merely to interpret or apply that framework to the situation in issue. His own philosophies are irrelevant. If in the opinion of the arbitrator the parties have written poor language, it is their responsibility and not his to change it. The test is not what is wise or what is sound industrial relations, but rather what is permissible under the terms of the agreement.

Some arbitrators, sensitive of this constraint, feel a responsibility to the parties to indicate to them the difficulty of resolving a given problem satisfactorily under the limited scope of their authority, and suggest that the problem might be more easily handled by direct negotiations. Thus, not infrequently, the arbitrator may bring about direct settlements rather than directed settlements. One should note, however, that a number of unions and managements alike regard this as meddling and prefer that the arbitrator retain his judicial function and not explore the possibility of settlements once the grievance procedure has been exhausted. The experienced arbitrator can usually sense or determine after superficial probing whether this additional help is desired or whether it would be considered out of order.

Unquestionably the greatest limitation on the scope of the arbitrator's authority is the fact that the arbitrator, and indeed the arbitration process, itself, are viable only to the extent that they continue to be acceptable to the parties. In the absence of compulsory arbitration, which is opposed by management, unions, and arbitrators, alike, neither the arbitrator nor the arbitration process is self-sustaining. There is nothing which requires the parties to select a particular arbitrator, and more important, nothing which requires the parties to continue to utilize arbitration as a future means of resolving grievance disputes. The greatly increased use of arbitration in the past twenty-five years, therefore, forces the conclusion that the arbitrator has carried out his function to render decisions within the limits of authority found generally acceptable to the parties.

To the arbitrator, beset by the conflicting economic and social philosophies of the respective parties, circumscribed by the terms of an often ambiguous collective bargaining agreement frequently made more ambiguous through the evolution of contrary practices, and faced with conflicting factual settings, the interpretation and application of the "common law of the shop" is not only a logical exercise of judicious reasoning, but also a fascinating experience in human relations.

CHAPTER 2

Arbitrability

The issue of arbitrability is the most basic issue which can be raised in arbitration because it is concerned with the authority of the arbitrator to hear or to decide a given dispute. Unlike other issues in which the parties attempt to convince the arbitrator of the merits of their respective positions, the issue of arbitrability questions the basic propriety of arbitration as the forum for the resolution of a given dispute. In effect, the party espousing a claim that the dispute is not arbitrable is arguing that irrespective of the merits of his opponent's position, the arbitrator has no right to hear or to decide the dispute. Indeed, it is not unusual for a party advancing such a claim to attempt to eliminate any discussion of the merits of the dispute until the arbitrability question has been resolved.

As arbitrability questions the basic propriety of the arbitration process for a given dispute, historically, more often than not, it was raised in the courts rather than before arbitrators. Courts frequently blurred the distinction between the issue of arbitrability and the merits of the case, and decided that an issue was not arbitrable merely because it lacked merit. In 1960 the Supreme Court in the *Steelworker Trilogy* rejected this approach and reduced the power of the federal courts to enjoin the arbitration of labor disputes.[1] Since that date the

---

[1] *United Steelworkers* v. *Enterprise Wheel & Car Corp.*, 363 U.S. 593 (1960); *United Steelworkers* v. *Warrior & Gulf Navigation Co.*, 363 U.S. 574 (1960); *United Steelworkers* v. *American Manufacturing Co.*, 363 U.S. 564 (1960).

distinction between the arbitrability of an issue and the merits of the issue has been more carefully maintained and the question of arbitrability has to a greater extent been placed in the hands of the arbitrator rather than argued before the courts.

THE ARBITRATION PROCESS

The authority of the arbitrator to hear and decide a dispute, in the normal instance, is derived from the collective bargaining agreement, itself, and is most commonly specifically spelled out in the grievance procedures of the agreement. Two quite common contract provisions governing the authority of the arbitrator are:

> Any dispute or grievance not settled according to the foregoing procedures may be submitted to arbitration.

> The arbitrator may interpret the agreement, but shall have no authority to alter or to modify the agreement.

While these provisions may seem clear on their face, they can raise a number of knotty problems.

One series of problems deals with procedural irregularities in the earlier steps of the grievance procedure. Many contracts require that grievances be filed within a certain time of the alleged violation. Does a failure to file within such a time limitation automatically disqualify such a grievance from being considered by the arbitrator, or do extenuating circumstances render such a grievance arbitrable? What extenuating circumstances should be considered? Further, how should time limits be treated in the case of a so-called "continuing violation" where the alleged violation is not one of a specific action limited in time, such as failure to pay the proper overtime for a given day's work, but rather one which may be repeated over and over such as the misclassification of an employee with consequent reduction of his hourly wage.

Frequently agreements also require the complaining employee to discuss the dispute with his foreman as a procedural prerequisite to the initiation of a formal grievance. In some cases these agreements make no provision for the so-called "policy grievance" or group grievance entered by the Union on behalf of large numbers of employees. Under these circumstances is a "policy grievance" arbitrable in the absence of a specific employee complainant and prior discussion with the foreman?

Another series of problems result from limitations on the arbitrator's authority to that of agreement interpretation. Usually these problems result from the nature of the subject matter itself. Where the subject matter is not mentioned in the contract, are grievances over these subjects arbitrable if the authority of the arbitrator is limited to that of interpreting the agreement? Thus, where there is no limitation on the right of discharge contained in the agreement, may a grievance alleging an unjust discharge be entertained in arbitration? Other subject matter frequently not explicitly treated in the agreement include Christmas bonuses, subcontracting, benefits under welfare programs, and the rights and obligations of supervisors.

Arbitrators must guard against either too liberal or too restrictive an approach to this issue. On the one hand, a propensity to find an issue arbitrable can fashion the arbitrator into the mold of an industrial witch-doctor, a meddler who assumes a decision-making role which neither his experience nor familiarity with company operations makes him competent to determine. Further, the arbitrator who too willingly assumes jurisdiction may unconsciously restrict the full exercise of collective bargaining by deciding issues that clearly should be left to the negotiating efforts of the parties themselves. Finally, if arbitration is to remain a truly voluntary process, no party should be forced to defend against a claim that he had no intention of submitting to an outside third party.

On the other hand, a reluctance to find an issue arbitrable can create equivalent problems. In effect, the arbitrator then denies the union the fullest expression of the grievance procedure, a procedure that has contributed much to the peaceful and orderly resolution of industrial disputes. Further, where the agreement contains a proscription against strikes and lockouts, arbitration performs an even greater service. It discharges the necessary task of resolving issues of contract interpretation where direct negotiations have failed, and the parties have agreed to eschew, for the life of the agreement, the use of economic force as an ultimate determinant.

CASES

1. The Jason Corporation Case

BACKGROUND OF THE CASE

On April 1, 1964, the union presented the company with a general written grievance claiming that some fifteen employees were not receiving their proper wages under the contract. The company refused to accept the grievance on the basis that it was a "shotgun grievance" and asked that, if there was a dispute over wages, individual grievances be submitted.

Immediately thereafter under date of April 3, 1964, the union submitted fifteen individual grievances written in an identical hand, but signed individually by the alleged grievants. Discussions were held between the company and the union on April 8, 1964 and April 15, 1964. No satisfactory settlement was reached and the union informed the company orally at the April 15, 1964 meeting of its intent to refer the dispute to arbitration.

At the arbitration hearing on August 19, 1964, the company refused to proceed on the merits of the dispute claiming nonarbitrability on grounds that the procedural steps of Article VII of the agreement had not been complied with.

APPLICABLE CONTRACT PROVISIONS

VII—Grievance Procedure

Disputes between the Company and the Union or between Company and the employee concerning the effect, interpretation, application, or claim of violation of the Agreement shall be settled in the following manner:

(a) If an employee has a complaint, he shall first confer promptly with his immediate superior and in any

event must confer within not more than two regularly
scheduled work days of the occurrence of the alleged
grievance.

(b) If the issue is not resolved within two regularly scheduled work days after presentation of the
matter to the immediate superior, the employee, together with the shop steward, shall confer with the
employee's immediate superior within five regularly
scheduled work days following the date of the occurrence. Grievance initiated in this manner will be stated
verbally.

(c) If a satisfactory settlement is not made within
three regularly scheduled work days succeeding the day
in which the grievance is submitted in accordance with
steps (b), the grievance shall be reduced to writing in
a grievance report in which the section of the agreement
allegedly violated shall be cited. This grievance report
shall be submitted by a Union representative to the
Company's superintendent within ten regularly scheduled
work days of the occurrence of the grievance. In the
event that a satisfactory settlement is not made in accordance with steps (c) within three regularly scheduled
work days after receipt of the grievance report by the
superintendent, the grievance may be presented for arbitration in accordance with the terms of this Agreement.

(d) Should the Company have a grievance, it shall
present the same in writing to the Union representative
within five regularly scheduled work days of the occurrence of the grievance, and if a satisfactory settlement
is not achieved within five regularly scheduled work days,
the grievance may be presented for arbitration in accordance with the terms of this Agreement.

(e) Should the aggrieved party or his representative,
as the case may be, fail to prosecute a grievance within
the time limits and in the manner and procedure above
described, the grievance shall be considered waived.

VIII—Arbitration

In the event that a grievance cannot be adjusted in accordance with the terms of the above Article, it shall be referred to arbitration with the arbitrator to be chosen by the

American Arbitration Association. However, any differences not referred to arbitration (or written notice of such desire to go to arbitration given) within forty-eight hours after the last meeting of the last step of a grievance procedure, shall be considered as settled. A decision of the arbitrator shall be final and binding upon both parties. The expense and salary of the arbitrator shall be borne by the party incurring them.

XIII Wages

This Agreement stipulates wage increases as follows: For all employees (with the exception of those covered by the supplemental agreement dated 27th of November 1961):

Effective December 15, 1962
.02 per hour increase
Effective June 1, 1963
.04 per hour increase

When an employee is hired he will, for the first sixty working days, be considered a probationary employee and for this period will be paid a probationary rate of wage. Upon completion of sixty working days he will be considered a permanent employee and will be paid the wage rate corresponding to the job to which he is assigned as set forth in this Agreement.

The following is a list of classifications together with the minimum rates applying thereto. It is to be understood that before the minimum rate can apply to any person that person must be qualified to actually do the work. The Company shall have 60 working days to determine the qualifications of the trainee.

GROUP I — 2.15/hr.
Pipe Machine Operators
Machinists
Electricians
Pattern Makers
Cupola Repair

GROUP II — 2.00/hr.
Molders—Day Work Molding
Machine Mechanics

GROUP III — 1.80/hr.
  Welders
  Auto Mechanics
  Iron Pourers—Pipe
  Wheelabrator Operators
  Core Machine Operators
  Muller Operator
  Crane Operator
  Iron Pourer—Fitting

GROUP IV — 1.71/hr.
  Laborers
  Cupola Helper and Tenders
  Cupola Chargers
  Shipping Loaders
  Bull Pushers
  Pipe Grinders
  Fitting Grinders

POSITION OF THE COMPANY

The company contends that the procedural requirements of the grievance procedure were not met, specifically Article VII, Section (a) which requires each employee having a complaint to confer first with his immediate supervisor before initiating a grievance.

Many of the employees who have signed the grievances at issue did not know what they were signing, and investigation disclosed that they were perfectly happy with their current wage rate. For these reasons, there is no arbitrable issue.

POSITION OF THE UNION

The union argues that under Article VII of the agreement it is not necessary in all cases to have an aggrieved party contact his supervisor. The company under Article VII, Section (d) has the right to initiate a grievance and the union also has that right both in the introductory language to Article VII, and also as a matter of simple equity.

Further, the union denies that the grievants are satisfied with their present wage rates under the company's interpretation of

Article XIII and that they were unaware of what they were signing when they formalized their respective grievances. Rather, the affected employees are inhibited when examined by company supervision and merely tell the company what it wants to hear in order to protect their jobs.

Finally, by entering into repeated discussions with the union on this issue, the company has, in effect, waived any right to contest the procedural inadequacy of the employees' grievances.

Suggested Discussion Questions

(a) If the agreement contained a no-strike, no-lockout clause, would this fact influence in any way an arbitrator's decision as to whether the issue was arbitrable? If so, specifically how would it influence an arbitrator's judgment?

(b) Would the fact that the agreement contained a clause which denied the arbitrator's authority "to change basic wage rates as set forth in this agreement" change your answer to the arbitrability of this grievance on the facts as announced? What other facts would you want to know?

(c) In what respect does the nature of the grievance, that is, the payment of proper wages, differentiate it from a grievance over disciplinary action from the standpoint of procedural requirements?

(d) Must the arbitrator determine whether the employees are dissatisfied with their wage rate in order to reach a finding on the arbitrability of the grievance? Why or why not?

2. The Larson Company Case

BACKGROUND OF THE CASE

In the spring of 1960, two shop stewards of the Extrusion Engineering Seniority area proposed an arrangement for changing the overtime procedures in that area. The foreman of the area requested that the stewards gain the consent of the affected employees, following which the proposal was presented to the company signed by more than 90 per cent of the active employees within that seniority area. The company studied the proposal and requested the following conditions which it set forth in writing:

For Consideration Before Attached Overtime Distribution System is Put Into Effect

1. Since support is not unanimous and it appears that the application will be a rather radical departure from the existing procedure, we should accept on a trial basis of approximately three months. At the end of this period, it might be desired to revert to the present procedure.

2. During the life of this modified procedure, it will be necessary for employees to accept supervision's word that attempts to contact employees were made in good faith.

3. At times that particular skills are needed, individuals possessing these skills may be asked without affecting any other employee's position on the overtime list.

4. Accessibility of employees need also be considered as reason for departing from call in, in strict accordance, with the overtime list. Example: A rush job is needed—a man near the plant might be called ahead of one who lives at a great distance.

5. No man will be asked to work overtime on the seventh day of the week.

These conditions were given to the shop stewards with the suggestion that they present these conditions and clarifications to the employees to determine whether the original proposal, as amended by the conditions and clarifications suggested by the company, was a satisfactory alternative to the existing procedure. The stewards reported that the overall arrangements were satisfactory, following which the revised overtime procedure was put into operation on April 27, 1960.

In accordance with this procedure, the company inquired of the union stewards at ninety-day intervals as to whether the arrangements were satisfactory. The last check was made on January 27, 1961. As a result of receiving assurances from the union representatives that there was no protest, and having received no protest from any other source, the company discontinued the periodic review and continued these arrangements.

In a grievance dated June 8, 1962, signed by Mr. Dewey A. Jackson (and signed later by some forty-odd other employees), the overtime procedure was attacked as follows:

> I am filing a grievance against Management for failing to distribute overtime in accordance with the Contract.

To which the company in the third step of the grievance procedure answered:

> Denied. Present side bar agreement for distribution of overtime is in accordance with the Contract.

In further grievance sessions the company indicated it would consider other overtime arrangements provided they were not contrary to existing principles of overtime, were practical, and were agreeable to the majority of employees in that seniority area. Growing out of these discussions a new proposal was submitted to the company, and it was agreed that a vote would be taken by the affected employees on the existing and the proposed overtime arrangements, as well as a third alternative in which employees could vote dissatisfaction with both of the proposals.

On December 12, 1962, the employees voted on the alternatives. Allegedly the union stewards and local union president reported to the company that the vote was inconclusive, although the existing procedure for overtime distribution received more votes than the new proposal. In view of this the union officers suggested that the existing procedure be continued and that, in view of the results, nothing further would probably be heard of the grievance.

On January 17, 1963, international officers of the union wrote the company offering to settle the grievance, as follows:

> As a result of this poll, the Union is agreeable to settle the grievance on the basis that overtime in the seniority area will be distributed in accordance with Article 5 of the Contract.

The company agreed to the above settlement provided that it contained the following additional clause: "except as modified by departmental agreements which are now in effect." This proviso not being acceptable to the union, it filed a demand for arbitration seeking the following remedy:

> That the Company comply with Article 5(G) of the Contract and distribute overtime in accordance therewith.

APPLICABLE CONTRACT PROVISIONS

Article 5

G. Overtime shall be distributed commencing in order of
    seniority as equally as practicable to all employees,
    but excluding those who have not yet earned seniority
    rating.

Article 21

D. Any time it is brought to the attention of either party
    that a grievance has been settled on a basis contrary
    to any provision of this Agreement, it shall be re-
    viewed by the Industrial Relations Department and
    full Union Grievance Committee, including Union
    representatives, and may be ratified by both parties
    or rejected by either.

POSITION OF THE COMPANY

The overtime arrangements of 1960 were duly bargained, accepted by both the company and the employees, and can be changed
only by collective bargaining. The arrangements were made completely independent of, and in the absence of any grievance from the
affected employees over the systems which prevailed prior to that
time. The procedure was administered for a period of over two
years without any complaint from any employee, including Dewey
A. Jackson, the grievant, who was subject to its terms.

While every opportunity was given to these employees to negotiate changes in the method of distributing overtime, they were
unable to decide upon any alternative. This leaves no alternative
but to rule that the system adopted in the spring of 1960 continues
in effect. Being in effect, it is beyond the scope of arbitration.

The issue is not concerned with the mechanics of administering
the system but is rather a protest concerning the use of the system
itself. Thus, there can be no question that the company has acted
in accordance with its duly negotiated agreement for the distribution
of overtime. To grant the requested relief would be to nullify a duly
bargained agreement and would thus exceed the accepted and historical scope of an arbitrator's authority. In essence, the union seeks

to void the 1960 overtime arrangement and substitute in lieu thereof Article 5(G) of the basic 1960 agreement. The company suggests there is no basis in fact or in the record to warrant such substitution without exceeding the powers conferred upon the arbitrator in his role as umpire of this dispute.

POSITION OF THE UNION

The union questions whether the arrangement of 1960 resulted in a binding agreement. The union points to the fact that the overall procedure, including the company's clarifications and conditions, is unsigned. Further, the union steward did not contact all employees in the seniority area to determine the acceptability of the company's conditions, but only those employees who signed the original proposal. In addition, the new arrangement under the company's own stipulated conditions was on a trial basis.

Even conceding, however, that the arrangement was a bona fide settlement, although the union does not so concede, then such a settlement was contrary to the terms of the existing agreement and may be rejected by either party under the provisions of Article 21(D) of the agreement. The so-called agreement violated the terms of Article 5(G) of the agreement in several important respects. First, no records were kept to indicate whether the company attempted to contact a given individual before calling in another. Secondly, the company established a rule whereby supervision could deprive a man of his turn in the case of rush jobs if he lived at any distance from the plant. Thirdly, another rule prevented a man from working the seventh day of the work week. These conditions made it impossible for overtime to be distributed in a fair and equal manner and therefore modified the contract language. The union had no knowledge of the settlement regarding the distribution of overtime in the area until the instant grievance was filed in June, 1962.

In the efforts made to resolve this dispute the parties agreed upon a poll conducted among the affected employees. The results of this poll indicate the employees' preference for distribution of overtime in accordance with Article 5(G) of the agreement.

(a) What reasons can you advance for the distinction made by the parties in the agreement between modifications to—and/or interpretations of—the agreement arising out of further negotiation and those made through grievance settlements? Does this distinction limit the "living document" theory of collective bargaining?

(b) Does the company's claim of nonarbitrability rest essentially upon the question of the merits of the dispute or that of the arbitrator's authority?

(c) Assuming that all of the company's contentions are found to be valid, does this mean that the dispute is therefore nonarbitrable? Explain.

(d) Does the side-bar agreement modify the provisions of the 1960 agreement? Explain.

3. The Kokomo Company Case

BACKGROUND OF THE CASE

The dispute giving rise to the demand for arbitration was a grievance phrased as follows:

Is it safe for one employee, in the bargaining unit, to perform work on the fifth floor of plant "N"?

The company, in a letter dated February 19, 1964, contested the arbitrability of the above grievance and at the hearing the parties agreed to confine their argument to the question of arbitrability. It was further agreed that a separate award and opinion should be addressed to this issue, and if the matter is deemed to be arbitrable, the arbitrator shall order the parties to proceed upon the merits.

APPLICABLE CONTRACT PROVISIONS

Article X

Section 2. In the event a grievance shall occur, such grievance in the first instance shall be taken up by the employee with his foreman.

Section 6. In the event that a grievance is not adjusted in accordance with the foregoing machinery, then either party shall have the right to submit the grievance to arbitration. In such event, either party may call upon the American Arbitration Association for the purpose of appointing an arbitrator. Neither party may be required to submit more than one (1) grievance to one (1) arbitrator at one (1) time.

The decision of the arbitrator shall be final, binding, and conclusive upon all parties. The arbitrator may interpret the agreement, but shall have no authority to alter or modify the same or any of the provisions thereof.

Article V

Section 1. Employees are expected to perform any reasonable duties to which they may be assigned.

POSITION OF THE COMPANY

Under Article X, Section 6 of the agreement, the authority of the arbitrator is restricted to that of interpreting the agreement. Since there is no provision of any kind in the agreement dealing with safety, such a matter is not subject to arbitration. Disputes over subjects not specifically covered by the agreement are not arbitrable if this silence is shown to be deliberate.

Silence with respect to safety issues has been deliberate. During the 1960 negotiations the union sought the following contract provision:

Item 26. A safety committee shall be established by the Company, and one man from the Union's Workmen's Committee shall serve on that Committee. The Chairman and Secretary of such Union Committee shall serve on the Safety Committee on a rotating basis.

During the 1962 negotiations the union made the following demand:

> Item 13. New Article: A Safety Committee of the Company
> and Union representatives shall inspect the plant at least
> once monthly. If the Company fails to correct any condi-
> tions reported by the Committee, the Union may refer such
> matters to the grievance procedure contained in the labor
> agreement and to arbitration.

During the 1963 negotiations, the union sought the following provision:

> 1. Whenever the Company assigns an employee to work
> on either night shift, there must be another person in
> the same building for safety purposes.

None of the above changes, however, was ever incorporated in the
agreement.

Although the term grievance as used in the agreement is not
defined, any such definition is unnecessary to the resolution of the
instant issue. The problem is whether the safety issue which has
been raised is an arbitrable matter, and the resolution of that issue
must be controlled primarily by the last sentence of Article X,
Section 6, which limits the arbitrator's authority to interpret the
agreement. The arbitrator is the creature of the parties and has
only those powers conferred on him by the parties. An arbitrator
can only interpret the contract as written. He cannot go into areas
on which the parties have been deliberately silent. The question of
whether an operation is safe or unsafe is a decision of the company,
or even a governmental inspection function, but not that of an arbitrator.

Article V, Section 1 of the agreement has no application to the
instant situation. There is no question about the work of the employee or about the reasonableness of the work or the duties. The
duties associated with the job are the same now as they have been
for many years, and no one has contended in the past and no one is
contending now that those duties are anything but reasonable. The
union is not suggesting or requesting any changes in the duties of
the job, but merely alleges that it is unsafe with one man. It is not
asking for more men. It is only seeking a declaration in answer to
a question of safety.

POSITION OF THE UNION

The instant issue is a narrow one; the union is merely asking the arbitrator to determine whether conditions are unsafe. The company accepted the grievance under the grievance procedure; it was processed through the various steps of the procedure; it was not until the grievance reached the terminal point that the company contested its arbitrability.

Safety conditions are a condition of employment, and Article I of the agreement recognizes the union as sole bargaining agent in these matters. Article V, Section 1 provides that "employees are expected to perform any reasonable duties to which they may be assigned." It is unreasonable to assign people to unsafe positions.

Under Article X, Section 2, there are no limitations on the subject matter of a grievance. Therefore, the company is obligated to process a grievance through the entire grievance procedure, a procedure which includes arbitration as its terminal point. It would have been a simple matter for the union to instruct the employees to refuse to perform the assignment because it was unsafe. Under these conditions there would be no question that any grievance resulting would be arbitrable. In the interests of harmonious relations, the union prefers to have the employees accept the assignment, albeit reluctantly, and process the claim through the grievance procedure. The union has every right to expect that safety hazards will be eliminated. Further, the union has the right to protest against unsafe conditions, and even the right to instruct employees to refuse to work under unreasonable conditions. While the union has other alternatives in the correction of unsafe conditions, the union may properly seek the determination of unsafe working conditions through arbitration.

Suggested Discussion Questions

(a) Suppose an arbitrator deems he has jurisdiction in this case, but that since the agreement is mute on safety, there is nothing for him to interpret. Would it not seem rather foolish for the arbitrator to hold the dispute arbitrable, to order the parties to go forward on the merits, and then to determine that he lacks authority to resolve the dispute?

(b) Can you think of any exceptions to the principle that disputes over subjects not specifically covered by the agreement are not arbitrable if this silence is shown to be deliberate?

(c) Do you think the union was wise in proceeding in the fashion it did rather than deciding on the alternative of refusing to work on grounds of "unsafe operations"?

Bibliography

Aaron, Benjamin, "Arbitration in the Federal Courts: Aftermath of the Trilogy," Collective Bargaining and the Arbitrator's Role, Proceedings of the Fifteenth Annual Meeting, National Academy of Arbitrators, Pittsburgh, Pa., January 24-26, 1962 (Washington, D. C.: Bureau of National Affairs, 1962), pp. 60-82.

Fleming, R. W., "Arbitrators and Arbitrability," Institute of Labor and Industrial Relations, Vol. LXI, No. 24 (October, 1963), pp. 220-221.

In re Celanese Corporation of America (Opinion of Arbitrator G. Allan Dash), 33 LA 925 (Washington, D. C.: Bureau of National Affairs).

Justin, Jules J., "Arbitrability and the Arbitrator's Jurisdiction," Management Rights and the Arbitration Process, Proceedings of the Ninth Annual Meeting, National Academy of Arbitrators, Cleveland, Ohio, January 26-28, 1956 (Washington, D. C.: Bureau of National Affairs, 1956), pp. 1-40.

Plaut, Frank, "Arbitrability Under the Standard Arbitration Clause," Arbitration Journal, Vol. XIV, No. 2 (1959), pp. 51-72.

Schmertz, Herbert, "When and Where the Issue of Arbitrability Can Be Raised," Industrial Relations - American Labor Arbitration, Vol. XXIII, Section 2, Report Bulletin No. 2 (July 23, 1962) (Englewood Cliffs, N. J.: Prentice-Hall, Inc., 1962).

Stone, Morris, Managerial Freedom and Job Security (New York, N. Y.: Harper & Row, Publishers, 1964), chap. i, "Introduction," pp. 1-21.

CHAPTER 3

Discipline

In the minds of many, the major role of the union in American society has been the protection of its members from the arbitrary decisions of management. Perhaps in no other area of management decision-making does this role become so dramatized as in that of industrial discipline. By the same token, with the advent of collective bargaining no other area of management decision-making has become so restricted and subject to third-party review and evaluation as management's imposition of discipline.

Paradoxically, unlike many other subjects legislated through collective bargaining, the labor agreement usually contains little in the way of arbitral guides for the resolution of disciplinary questions. Many agreements provide no more than a bare statement that "employees shall not be discharged except for 'just cause.'" Does this then mean that employees may be assessed lesser disciplinary measures without the need for just cause? Moreover, what is meant by just cause? Usually the answer to this question involves the arbitrator in two other major questions: first, is the employee guilty of an infraction meriting disciplinary action; secondly, is the penalty proper under all the circumstances.

In determining whether the employee is guilty of an offense, the arbitrator becomes, in effect, a fact-finder. There are, however, important differences between the arbitrator's role in this area and that of a jury under our civil and criminal legal system. Unlike the jury which, as a body, is presumed to have no knowledge of evidence, the

24

arbitrator, as both judge and juror, must determine what facts to consider and what weight to give those facts. Are the facts relevant and to what extent? Should hearsay evidence be admitted and what weight should it be given? It is in disciplinary cases, particularly, that the informality of the arbitration process, unshackled by the legal restrictions on evidence, may come into conflict with the rights of the accused, commonly referred to as due process. Does the presumption of innocence follow the accused employee into the arbitration hearing? If so, what burden of proof must the employer shoulder in order to justify his disciplinary action?

Nor do company rules have the force of community laws in at least several respects: their reasonableness is subject to question, and ignorance of them may be excused if management has not communicated them to the work force, or if by its actions it has patently neglected to enforce them. Entrapment obviously has no place in the employer-employee relationship. Thus, the arbitrator must determine the following questions. Is the rule reasonable? Was it properly communicated to the employees? Has it been consistently applied to the work force? If not, does its application to the accused employee amount to discriminatory treatment?

In determining the propriety of the penalty, the old saw that the "penalty must fit the crime" is an oft-used but relatively useless criterion. More basic is to what extent should the arbitrator substitute his judgment for that of management, once he has found the accused employee guilty? Obviously, when the penalty can be shown to be arbitrary, discriminatory, and capricious. Thus, two other questions may be raised. What penalty has the employer exacted in similar situations in the past? Are extenuating circumstances present in the case at issue which make comparison with past situations unrealistic and unfair?

The lack of arbitral guides in the collective bargaining agreement for the resolution of disciplinary questions, and the fact-finding nature of the arbitral function in these questions lead to a wide range of arbitrators' views on matters of discipline. Given similar factual situations, arbitrators would, in all likelihood, disagree as to the degree of guilt or the propriety of a given disciplinary penalty. One might argue that, in this area, it is the mature judgment of the arbitrator, rather than his analytical ability to interpret contract language, which is sought by the parties in dispute.

CASES

4. The Foster Motor Freight Company Case

BACKGROUND OF THE CASE

Mr. Leonard Wilcox was employed by the Foster Motor Freight Company as a truck driver on May 1, 1947. From that date until June 16, 1962, his work record showed that he had never been involved in a serious accident. On June 16, 1962, while at the wheel of a company truck, he was involved in a catastrophic accident which resulted in the death of four persons, injuries to five others, and considerable property damage. As a result, he was indicted by the grand jury for involuntary manslaughter and placed under bail for his appearance in county court.

After several conversations between union and company representatives, the company agreed to return Mr. Wilcox to driving a truck, restricting him only to driving within the state, pending his trial in county court. It was further understood that the entire matter would be reviewed by company and union officials after the completion of Mr. Wilcox' trial.

Mr. B. L. Foster, manager of Foster Motor Freight Company, attended the trial and, after hearing the prosecution's case, testified under oath for the defendant. Transcript of the trial shows that he stated: "Leonard Wilcox is one of our best employees." He further testified that "if Leonard Wilcox doesn't lose his truck driver's license, we will retain him in our employ as a truck driver."

Mr. Wilcox was convicted of involuntary manslaughter and was sentenced to a prison term, but the sentence was immediately suspended by the court. The grievant's license to drive a truck was not revoked by the state.

Immediately thereafter, the company discharged Mr. Wilcox on the basis of his responsibility for the accident as determined by the county court. Mr. Wilcox then filed a grievance protesting his discharge, contending that the company discharged him without justifiable cause and requesting his reinstatement with full seniority rights and restitution of all monies lost by reason of his discharge. No satisfactory settlement was reached by the parties, and the union filed a demand for arbitration.

APPLICABLE CONTRACT PROVISIONS

Article 10—Section 1

The Company shall have the right to discipline an employee for justifiable cause.

POSITION OF THE COMPANY

The company argues that there can be no question of just cause for discharge since the county court found the grievant guilty of criminal negligence. The mere fact that the court suspended his prison sentence in no way dilutes the court's findings. Moreover, as a result of this negligence, four persons were killed, five others were injured, and considerable loss of property resulted.

The action of the grievant also subjected the company to damage suits amounting to many hundreds of thousands of dollars, not to mention the loss of its truck and trailer. Though it is covered by insurance, its insurance rates for future liability coverage will increase considerably as a result of the grievant's negligence, and retention of the grievant is likely to cause them to rise even more.

Moreover, the company has a responsibility to the public at large. The public should not be subjected to the hazard of encountering a negligent truck driver on the highway. The company's responsibility in this regard is all the greater by reason of its knowledge that the grievant's negligence caused the catastrophic accident which gives rise to this case. The incident undoubtedly has also reduced the competence of the grievant with respect to future driving, since he will always carry with him the grim memory of his past negligent action.

The company made no agreement with the union to maintain the grievant in its employ. Rather, it agreed to review the situation after the outcome of the court case. The verdict of involuntary manslaughter returned by the jury released the company from any further obligation to maintain the grievant in its employ.

The company is unaware of any industry practice which would prevent it from discharging a driver before involvement in three chargeable accidents. Nor can it be bound by such practice in the absence of evidence that it agreed to be bound. The company further submits that in its twenty-year history none of its drivers has ever been found guilty of criminal negligence in an accident. Regardless of the grievant's prior record, this fact alone constitutes just cause for discharge.

POSITION OF THE UNION

The union contends that industry practice is not to discharge a truck driver on the basis of one accident, but that three chargeable accidents normally constitute basis for discharge. The company is aware of this practice and is bound by it. Under this standard the grievant's record is not one which merits his discharge, since he was never previously involved in a chargeable accident.

The testimony under oath of the company's manager at the grievant's trial estops the company from subsequently claiming that it had justifiable cause for his discharge, since the license of the grievant was not revoked by the state. Furthermore, the manager testified under oath that the grievant was "one of our best employees." This statement occurred after the accident and, indeed, after all of the prosecution's testimony had been revealed at the grievant's trial.

The agreement between company and union representatives to permit the grievant to return to his job pending the trial of his case was not intended by the parties to make the decision reached in the trial determinative of his right to continued employment with the company. It was merely agreed that the parties would again meet and discuss his future status with the company following the trial and after a careful review of all the circumstances bearing on the case. No restrictions were placed on the driving of the grievant during this interim period, except the restriction of driving only within the state, a restriction required by the conditions of his bail bond. Under these circumstances, the mere fact that the grievant was convicted of involuntary manslaughter as a result of his one unfortunate accident does not constitute justifiable cause for discharge.

(a) Should "past practice" have a bearing upon the present case, and under what conditions?

(b) Does the arbitrator have a responsibility to protect the interest of the "public" in reaching his decision in a case of this nature? Does the state have a similar responsibility?

(c) Suppose that the grievant had been involved in two previous accidents in the first of which no one was injured, but property damage resulted, and in the second of which one person was injured, although not seriously, but there was slight property damage involved. Would this constitute just cause for his present discharge?

(d) What significance would you attach to the fact that the company permitted him to drive a truck upon his recovery from his injuries in the fatal accident?

(e) Suppose the accident, indictment, and trial giving rise to the above issue arose out of the grievant's negligence in his own car and outside of company working hours. Would this change your opinion? Explain fully.

5. The Cordon Manufacturing Company Case

BACKGROUND OF THE CASE

During World War II, the Cordon Manufacturing Company was engaged in the production of war materials. Certain hand assembly operations were required which were carried out by female assemblers who were seated on both sides of a moving belt which both supplied them with the parts and carried away the finished product.

Patricia Kelly had been working on the assembly line since its inception. A quiet and reserved person, she was well liked by her co-workers. She was married to a soldier a few days before he was sent into combat in the Pacific theatre of operations. For some four months previous to the incident out of which the instant grievance arose, she had suddenly stopped receiving letters from her husband,

which situation, when combined with the newspaper casualty reports
from that area, had caused her to become quite despondent. Most
of her co-workers sympathized with her condition and tried without
success to cheer her up.

Seated immediately across the assembly belt from Mrs. Kelly
was Florence Lacey who had been employed by the company as an
assembler for approximately two months. Miss Lacey was a well-
shaped blonde who blatantly advertised her charms in extremely
tight sweaters and gaily colored skin-tight slacks. She had dis-
pensed her favors not without success on a number of male employees of the company in her brief period of employment. Her
morals and attitude were such that she was cordially hated by most
of her female co-workers.

For the past few months overtime on the assembly line had increased to the point where the line was working fifty-six hours per
week. On the morning of April 25, 1944, Miss Lacey announced in
a loud voice: "I don't know how you gals feel about it, but the overtime is wonderful. I ain't never had it so good—I hope it continues
forever." At this point, Mrs. Kelly stood up, reached across the
assembly line, grabbed Miss Lacey by the hair, shook her head
vigorously, and punched her in the face. The punch in the face
sent Miss Lacey sprawling upon the floor.

Mrs. Kelly immediately went to the lockerroom and dressed to
leave the plant. Upon leaving the lockerroom she was approached
by her foreman who told her that he had witnessed the entire scene
from the other end of the department, some seventy feet distant.
He pointed out that under the company rules and regulations he had
no choice but to discharge her for fighting during working hours.
He pointed out that he was particularly sorry he had to take this
action, for Mrs. Kelly had been an excellent worker with an un-
blemished record. At the direction of the foreman, she reported
to the payroll office, collected her pay, and left the plant.

That same evening her shop steward visited her and informed
her that many of the girls on the assembly line were upset about
her discharge and that he had great difficulty in preventing them
from "pulling a wildcat strike." He asked her what had happened,
and she related the facts set forth above. She reported that she
was so worried about her husband's safety that at Miss Lacey's
remarks she lost all her self-control. She added that she was
aware of the company rule against fighting and realized the company
had no recourse except to discharge her.

The shop steward informed her that he had taken the matter up
with the foreman, but that the foreman insisted that Mrs. Kelly was
the aggressor. The foreman also quoted the company rule which
provided:

> Any employee who physically strikes another employee ex-
> cept in self-defense during working hours shall be subject
> to immediate discharge.

The shop steward pointed out, however, that many of the girls on
the assembly line had heard the remarks of Miss Lacey and felt
that Mrs. Kelly was completely justified in doing what she did under
the circumstances. In fact, he told Mrs. Kelly that if she would
not file a grievance demanding her reinstatement, he had been instructed by the other girls to file one for her on behalf of the union.

The shop steward finally persuaded Mrs. Kelly to file a grievance protesting her discharge, and when the company refused to
change its position, the union appealed the matter to arbitration.

APPLICABLE CONTRACT PROVISIONS

Article X—Management Rights

The Company shall have the right to make all reasonable rules and regulations that are deemed necessary to
regulate the conduct of its employees while they are on
the premises of the Company.

Article XIV—Discipline

The Company shall not discharge or terminate any
employee from the employ of the Company except for
just cause.

POSITION OF THE COMPANY

The company contends that under the agreement it has the right
to establish reasonable rules and regulations. It has established a
rule making fighting, except in self-defense, a dischargeable offense and has strictly enforced this rule since its inception. The
grievant was aware of such a rule, and as the admitted aggressor
clearly violated this rule. For these reasons the action of the
company must be upheld.

POSITION OF THE UNION

The union contends that it has never agreed to be bound by the rules unilaterally established by the company. Although it admits that the company has discharged other employees for fighting on company premises, without protest by the union, it insists that the company has never before discharged an employee under the extreme provocation which was present in the instant case. The union points out that standards of equity demand that the company take into consideration the extremely selfish nature of the remarks, the type of person who made them, and the nervous strain that Mrs. Kelly was under at the time the remarks were made. In short, the union urges that the remarks, in themselves, were extreme provocation and that any reasonable person would have reacted as did Mrs. Kelly.

Suggested Discussion Questions

(a) Does the company unilaterally have the right to make rules and regulations concerning the conduct of its employees, which, if violated, may result in disciplinary action?

(b) Suppose Mrs. Kelly had restrained her anger during working hours, but had accosted Miss Lacey immediately after work and off the company premises. Under these circumstances, would the company have reasonable grounds for disciplining Mrs. Kelly?

(c) Suppose Mrs. Kelly had not encountered her foreman upon leaving the lockerroom, but had proceeded out of the plant. Under these circumstances, could it be said that she was a voluntary quit?

(d) Did Mr. Brown, Mrs. Kelly's foreman, make a sufficient investigation of the circumstances that led up to her actions?

(e) Would a decision in favor of the grievant "open the door" to assaults by one employee upon another on company premises?

6. The De Forest Corporation Case

BACKGROUND OF THE CASE

The De Forest Corporation is engaged in the manufacture and sale of corrugated paper products. Mr. George Gamely, the grievant, was employed by the company on March 1, 1940 as a laborer. At the time of the present incident he was classified as a tow-truck operator whose duty it was to pick up quantities of corrugated paperboard with his large fork-lift truck and transport them from the corrugators to the pressroom. On September 8, 1964, Mr. James Kerns, press foreman, observed the tow-truck being driven by the grievant in reverse, turning the corner from the corrugators into the pressroom. Allegedly, the fork lifts were three feet off the floor and the corrugated paperboard measuring 35" x 90" was stacked five and one-half feet high on a pallet resting on the fork lift. As the tow-truck reached the number one press the load of corrugated paperboard started to slide off the truck. Nevertheless, the grievant did not stop the tow-truck until it reached the number three press, a distance of thirty feet. In consequence, over three hundred pieces of corrugated paperboard were strewn in the aisle from the number one press to the number three press, some of which blocked the rail line between these three presses and caused the number two and number three presses to shut down until that line was unblocked. When Mr. Kerns arrived on the scene, the grievant was standing on his tow-truck with his hands in his pockets, whereupon Mr. Kerns said to him, "Come on George, let's get this cleaned up." The grievant then said, "The Hell with you and the paperboard too." By this time Mr. Sparton, the press supervisor, arrived at the scene and instructed the grievant to help clean up the mess and get the rails clear so that the number two and number three presses could operate, to which he received the same reply as had Mr. Kerns, plus the statement that they could get a helper to do that work and that it was not his job to do it. Thereupon, Mr. Sparton instructed the grievant to assist in clearing away the paperboard or he would have to take drastic disciplinary action. The grievant replied, "The Hell with you both, I'm astandin' on my rights."

Messrs. Kerns, Sparton, and a helper cleared away the paperboard from the rails, and the number two and number three presses returned to operation. Mr. Sparton then walked over to where the grievant was standing beside his tow-truck and said: "George, since you refused to obey the instructions of Mr. Kerns and myself, I have no recourse but to discharge you. Get your pay." Mr. Sparton then returned to his office, called in the grievant's shop steward, informed him as to what had happened, and filled out a disciplinary notice with the grievant's name upon it stating: "You are discharged as of 10:30 A. M. for insubordination, disobedience of orders, and use of profanity."

On September 9, 1964, the grievant filed a grievance demanding that he "be reinstated to his job, tow-truck operator, without loss of seniority and made whole for any loss of pay."

On Saturday, September 2, 1954, while the plant was operating, but the grievant was not scheduled to work, he, two other men, and three women walked into the plant in an hilarious mood, with the odor of intoxicating liquor on their breaths, and without authority. They had to be ejected by the use of some force by the plant guards, which commotion caused the company a loss of production. For that offense the grievant was discharged. However, because of the strong plea of the union business agent that the incident occurred over the Labor Day weekend when some employees tend to imbibe too much, and because of the grievant's spotless record, the company converted the discharge to a three-day disciplinary suspension, accompanied by the following written warning:

1. That you will never again enter the plant except when scheduled to work, without permission from your supervisor.

2. That you will never report for work with the smell of liquor on your breath.

3. That the breach by you of any plant rule in the future will result in your immediate discharge.

The grievant mended his ways until 1962 when on several Fridays (the day after pay day) he was absent from work, and on several other Fridays his supervisor detected the odor of liquor on his breath. On each of those occasions he was orally reprimanded by his foreman, Mr. Kerns.

The grievance in the instant case was processed through the required steps of the grievance procedure, but the parties were unable to reach a satisfactory settlement, whereupon the union appealed the grievance to arbitration.

APPLICABLE CONTRACT PROVISIONS

Article 14

The Company shall have the . . . right to make reasonable rules and regulations . . . and it shall have the right to discipline or discharge an employee for justifiable cause.

The company unilaterally established a set of rules and regulations in 1952 which set up a series of minor violations and major violations, with attendant penalties for their breach. Minor violations provided for an oral warning for the first violation, a written warning for the second violation, and discharge for a third violation. Among these violations were: excessive lateness and absenteeism, horseplay, reading a newspaper or other material not connected with the employee's work, and having the odor of intoxicating liquor on one's breath during working hours. Major violations included among others, dishonesty, imbibing of alcoholic beverages while on duty, entering the company premises without permission, insubordination, and physically assaulting or cursing a supervisor. The company was empowered to discharge an employee for his first infraction of a major violation.

POSITION OF THE COMPANY

The company contended that Mr. John Horn, a shop steward in a department continguous to the pressroom, had informed Mr. Sparton about a minute before the load of paperboard slipped from the grievant's tow-truck that he detected the odor of alcoholic beverage on the grievant's breath, and questioned whether the safety of co-workers might be jeopardized. Moreover, the company further contended that when Messrs. Kerns and Sparton talked with the grievant, they detected such an odor on his breath. This evidence, coupled with the fact that the fork lift of the tow-truck was three feet off the plant floor was evidence at least of carelessness. In addition, the company pointed out that the grievant did not stop his tow-truck until it had

traversed thirty feet from the place that the load started to slip. Mr.
Kerns testified that nothing was wrong with the tow-truck brakes because Mr. Jordan, the helper who operated it for the balance of the
shift after the grievant was discharged, had no difficulty in stopping it
within a distance of three feet from the time that he applied the brakes.

The company submitted that it had been more than lenient in reinstating the grievant after his discharge for the September 2, 1954
incident, and at that time gave him a written warning that any subsequent infraction of the company's rules and regulations would result in his discharge. It also pointed out that although the grievant
had not caused any trouble between 1954 and 1962, he had been absent
without reporting off on several days after pay day, and on several
other such days his foreman had detected the odor of intoxicating
liquor on his breath when he came to work, but recognizing that he
was not actually intoxicated had been generous and had given him
only oral warnings.

The company insisted that both Mr. Kerns and Mr. Sparton had
instructed the grievant to assist in removing the paperboard, which
had slipped from his tow-truck, so that the number two and number
three presses could resume operation, and that not only did he refuse to do so, but that he used abusive and cursing language in his
refusal. In consequence, the company urges that such actions constituted both insubordination and the use of cursing language in ad-
dressing a supervisor, both of which constitute major violations
under the company's rules and regulations. Therefore, the company
requests that the arbitrator, for the above stated reasons, find that
the company had justifiable cause for discharging the grievant on
September 8, 1964.

POSITION OF THE UNION

The union did not have any witnesses testify at the arbitration
hearing; its legal counsel presented the union's case in the form of
oral argument. He pointed out the seriousness of the discharge of
an employee, particularly one who has twenty-four years of service
with the company and is fifty-eight years of age. Moreover, he submitted that the company recognized that the discharge of the grievant
in 1954 was too severe a penalty; in fact that it was actually nothing
more than a prank by an exuberant employee who meant no harm
and did not enter the company's premises to steal anything. Furthermore, the union contended that the company's written warning upon

the grievant's reinstatement in 1954 was too severe in that it made
him dischargeable for the slightest cause thereafter. Union counsel
supported this contention by pointing to the fact that on several occasions in 1962, Mr. Kerns had detected the odor of intoxicating
liquor on the grievant's breath very shortly after he had reported for
work and yet did nothing more than give him an oral reprimand, but
still permitted him to drive his tow-truck for the balance of ths shift.
Moreover, the union argued that the grievant's overall past record has
been reasonably good and that his few errant actions should not be permitted to hand like "the sword of Damocles" over his head forever.

Union counsel then contended that actually the grievant was not
being insubordinate because he honestly believed that it was not a
part of the duties of his job classification to clear the rails of spilled
paperboard, but that it was the duty of the helper to perform this
work. As a consequence, he believed that by assisting Messrs.
Kerns and Sparton he would be depriving the helper of work that belonged to him. In addition, if the company's allegation is correct
that the grievant had the odor of intoxicating liquor on his breath,
which the union contends was not proven by any tests, then that
condition would prove that he actually had no premeditated intention
of being insubordinate.

Lastly, union counsel urged that the arbitrator must take into
consideration that this is a paper mill and that the language used
therein is commonly not that which would be used in high society.
In short, that the words, "the Hell with you" are not considered
to amount to cursing in a mill of this kind.

Union counsel urged the arbitrator to order the company to reinstate the grievant to his job classification, tow-truck operator,
without loss of seniority and with at most a five-day disciplinary
suspension.

Suggested Discussion Questions

(a) Is there a distinction between insubordination and disobedience
of orders ?

(b) Under any circumstances may an employee refuse to obey an
order of his supervisor ?

(c) Should the company's evidence of the grievant's past record be
considered by the arbitrator in arriving at his decision in the
present arbitration ?

(d) Should the arbitrator be influenced by the company's past action
     in dealing with the grievant's violation of company rules?

7. The Appleton Company Case

BACKGROUND OF THE CASE

Mr. James Tilton, the aggrieved employee, was hired by the
company in July, 1948 as a laborer and continued to work in that
job classification until December, 1949 when he was laid off in line
of seniority because of lack of work. He entered the Armed Services
and upon his discharge therefrom was taken back by the company in
February, 1951 in the same job classification. On April 30, 1951
he was reclassified to the job classification, processor—chips and
oil. Between the time that the grievant re-entered the service of
the company and his subsequent reclassification he had been reprimanded orally by his foreman twice for horseplay. Subsequent to
his reclassification he had been reprimanded orally on ten occasions
for somewhat similar tactics; six times by his foreman, twice by his
department head, and twice by the night superintendent. Each of the
last ten oral reprimands carried with it an oral warning that his
actions were in violation of a company rule and that his next rule
violation would result in his discharge.

Among the pranks which the grievant perpetrated was that of
snapping an oil-soaked rag, especially when he was near an employee who had stooped over to pick up a piece of material. In addition, he found Tony Garcia, a fifty-four year old machine operator
of Italian extraction, a particularly susceptible victim of his pranks,
such as putting sand in his bologna sandwich when he was not looking,
and tieing the shoelaces of Tony's extra pair of work shoes into many
knots, after wetting the laces.

The twelfth oral warning seemed to have served its purpose for
over two months, but on April 1, 1952 the grievant observed Tony
Garcia, with his feet propped up resting his aching bunions, taking
a short nap during his lunch hour. The grievant could not resist
the temptation and stealthily placed a large stick match alongside
of the welt of Tony's shoe, lit it, and then quickly departed into the
nearby stock room. In stamping out the burning match Tony struck

one of his bunions and in rage set out to find the grievant. Just as
the siren ending the lunch period sounded, he encountered Mr.
Walsh, the night superintendent, and angrily informed him that he
would take matters into his own hands if the grievant continued to
make his life miserable. Mr. Walsh replied that he had observed
the incident from some distance and that Tony need not worry further
because this was the "last straw" and that he personally would discharge Jim Tilton immediately.

Mr. Walsh went to the grievant's work station where he found
him diligently at work. He informed him that he had observed his
latest prank and that the company had a rule prohibiting horseplay;
that the grievant had been guilty of violating it on twelve previous
occasions, the last ten of which had been accompanied by a warning
of discharge. In consequence, he explained to the grievant that he
had no recourse other than to discharge him, even though otherwise
he had been a good worker, so "This is it, you are discharged."
The grievant punched out his time card, got his pay, but then talked
with his shop steward, and as a result filed a grievance demanding
reinstatement to his job, without loss of seniority, and with full
compensation for any time which he might lose as a result of the
discharge.

The grievance was duly processed through the various steps of
the grievance procedure, but the company staunchly maintained
that its action was proper. In consequence, the union appealed the
grievance to arbitration.

APPLICABLE CONTRACT PROVISIONS

XIII—Management Rights

The Company shall have the right to . . . make
reasonable rules and regulations governing the conduct
of its employees while they are at work in the plant or
on Company premises . . . .

In 1945 the company unilaterally established a set of company
rules and regulations, which it published in booklet form, and supplied each existing employee and every employee hired subsequent
thereto with a copy. This set of rules and regulations established
major violations and minor violations. For infraction of the former
the company could discharge an employee for his first violation.

For the latter he was entitled to two warnings prior to his discharge for a third violation. Among the minor violations was a provision: "No employee shall be permitted to engage in 'horseplay' during working hours or while on Company premises."

POSITION OF THE COMPANY

The company contended that Article XIII of the labor agreement gave it the exclusive right to make reasonable rules and regulations governing the conduct of its employees while they are at work in the plant or while on the company's premises. Moreover, the company contended that it supplemented that Article in 1945 by establishing a set of reasonable rules and regulations, which it furnished to all existing and all new employees of the company, a copy of which the personnel file of the grievant shows that he received upon being hired.

Furthermore, the company insists that said rules and regulations are reasonable because they distinguish between major and minor violations, with the right to mete out discharge for the first offense of a major violation, but not to discharge an employee for a minor violation until he has been guilty of a third minor violation.

In addition, the company argued that no contention has been made by the grievant or the union that the grievant did not commit thirteen violations of the rule prohibiting horseplay, which is a rule that is necessary if the company is to be able to conduct its operations without utter chaos in the plant. Also, on each of the prior twelve occasions he had been given adequate warning that his next minor violation would result in his discharge. In consequence, the company argued strenuously that the grievant had been given every possible "break" and that there "comes a time when it must take positive action and can do no less than to discharge the offending employee under the circumstances."

POSITION OF THE UNION

The union pointed out that the company's rules and regulations were established unilaterally by the company. Moreover, the union argued that it had successfully challenged the administration of some of said rules and regulations on a few occasions by taking the company's action to arbitration. It also argued that discharge is the equivalent of capital punishment in industrial society and should be meted out only as a last resort. In substantiation of this position it insisted that the company should have taken into consideration that the grievant is only twenty-two years of age, is married and has four children, and had served in the Armed Forces where "horseplay" is a common occurrence and that none of his pranks were designed to cause bodily injury to another employee, nor was there evidence that any resulted in same.

Furthermore, the union argued that the company failed to meet reasonably its obligation in enforcing its rules and regulations and, in consequence, the grievant should be reinstated to his job without loss of seniority, and be made whole for any monetary loss which he sustained as a result of his discharge.

Suggested Discussion Questions

(a) Did the company have the unilateral right to establish whatever rules and regulations it saw fit to establish?

(b) Did the company follow the doctrine of "constructive discipline" in the administration of its rules and regulations?

(c) Should the age of the grievant, his family status, his Armed Services career, and his record otherwise as a "good employee" be taken into consideration by the arbitrator in arriving at his decision?

(d) If the case is decided in favor of the grievant, would this set a precedent regarding "horseplay," and if so, is there anything that the company could do unilaterally to protect the company in the future from unbridled "horseplay"?

(e) As the arbitrator, in your decision would you recommend that a "statute of limitations" be established which would enable an employee to clear his record after the lapse of a certain period of time in which he did not violate a minor violation rule?

8. The Cole Company Case

BACKGROUND OF THE CASE

Mr. Edward Dembow is a filler on the sulphuric acid packaging line of the company's operations. Because of the danger from contact with acid, all employees on this line wear protective clothing, For example: gloves, sleeves, aprons, goggles, and boots, furnished by the company. Allegedly the company was having some difficulty in getting its workers to be properly dressed in protective clothing ready to start work at 8:00 A.M., the normal starting hour. This was particularly serious with respect to the filler, since he occupies the first position on the packaging line and all other work on the line follows in sequence.

On October 7, 1964, Mr. Sidney Lester, president of the company, allegedly warned Mr. Dembow approximately ten minutes before the starting hour that he expected him to be ready to start work by 8:00 A.M. Mr. Lester visited the line again at 8:00 A.M. and believing that Mr. Dembow was not properly dressed and ready for work told him that he was docking him fifteen minutes pay for not being ready to start work at the regular starting hour. Apparently little, if any, work was accomplished since Mr. Lester returned in a few minutes and threatened to dock the entire shop if the employees did not begin work. He returned again in a few minutes and found Mr. Dembow sitting on an empty packing case some twenty-five feet away from his normal position on the sulphuric acid line. He ordered Mr. Dembow to start work, but the latter replied that he would not start working "on his own time," but would wait until the fifteen minutes were up. Mr. Lester then discharged Mr. Dembow.

On October 12, 1964, the company and the union tried to reach a settlement, but the terms of the settlement, namely reinstatement without back pay, were not acceptable to Mr. Dembow and the union demanded arbitration of the issue.

On October 14, 1964, the company wrote the grievant a letter which read, in part:

> You are hereby notified that you have been given an 8-day suspension without pay for repeated failure to begin work

promptly. You are hereby notified to return to work on
Friday, October 16, 1964.

The grievant returned to work on that date and the union is seeking
a determination of the propriety of the disciplinary suspension.

APPLICABLE CONTRACT PROVISIONS

Article 10—Discharges

(a) The right of the Company to discharge for just
cause is acknowledged.

(b) The Company shall have the absolute right to
discharge temporary employees as defined in Article 6.

(c) A discharge shall not be the subject of adjustment of grievance under Article 9 unless written notice
is filed with a Company representative within forty-eight
(48) hours of such discharge. The forty-eight (48) hour
period shall not include Saturdays, Sundays, or Holidays
set forth in this agreement.

(d) If reinstatement is ordered as a result of the
grievance procedure under Article 9 or the arbitration
procedure under Article 11 of this agreement, the order
of reinstatement shall provide whether it is with or without pay for days lost, but in no event shall the Company
be liable for more than the equivalent of ninety (90) work
days' wages at the employee's regular rate of pay.

POSITION OF THE UNION

The alleged warnings given to the grievant were not warnings,
but merely suggestions to all employees on the sulphuric acid line
that they should be ready to start work at 8:00 A.M. At no time
were the employees specifically warned that disciplinary action
would be taken for failure to start work promptly at 8:00 A.M.
Each employee is clearly entitled to know when he is being warned
so that he may have an opportunity to correct his actions before
serious discipline is imposed.

The company in the person of Mr. Lester did discipline the
grievant when he docked him fifteen minutes of wages for not being
ready to begin work promptly at 8:00 A.M. The refusal of the

grievant to work during a period in which the company had refused
to pay him does not amount to a wildcat strike, but is merely the
normal reaction of an employee when wages are withheld. Therefore, the discharge of the grievant, which was later moderated by
the substitution of an eight-day suspension, was improper, and the
grievant should be compensated for all time lost.

POSITION OF THE COMPANY

Although the position of the company is that the actions leading
up to the instant issue were the result of a show of strength by each
party, the matter of causation is irrelevant, and the narrow issue
is whether the grievant was ready to perform his work at 8:00 A. M.

Contrary to the union's contention, a number of warnings had
been given by the company over this issue in the past, and certainly
on the day in question. Mr. Edward Dembow was specifically warned
only ten minutes previous to the incident giving rise to this dispute.

The company agrees that discharge was too severe a penalty and
as a result it substituted a more moderate disciplinary action. Despite disagreement by the parties over the length of the disciplinary
suspension assessed, the conduct of the grievant certainly called for
some disciplinary action, and an eight-day disciplinary suspension
was not too harsh a penalty.

Suggested Discussion Questions

(a) The company suggests that the discipline assessed was for the
     offense of not being ready to start at 8:00 A. M. Yet the grievant
     had moments earlier to his discharge already been assessed a
     disciplinary penalty of fifteen minutes docking of his pay. Does
     this imply a dual penalty for the same offense? Does such action
     constitute double jeopardy? Explain carefully giving reasons for
     your position.

(b) Strangely enough neither party raises the issue of insubordi-
     nation although the factual situation indicates that this was in
     essence the reason for the grievant's discharge. Do you think
     the parties' avoidance of this aspect was an oversight or in-
     tentional stemming from a concern on the part of each party
     that opening up of this issue might prove detrimental to its
     position? Explain.

(c) The union raises the wildcat strike issue as a straw-man
     argument. How would you distinguish insubordination from a
     wildcat strike ?

(d) During cross-examination of Mr. Lester, the union asked
     whether he had not been advised by his attorney on the day of
     the discharge to put the grievant back to work as quickly as
     possible. The company attorney objected to this question on
     the grounds that it was privileged conversation. As an arbi-
     trator would you uphold the objection ? Suppose later on in
     presenting rebuttal testimony the international representative
     of the union testified that the company attorney had indicated
     to him during the grievance meeting of October 12, 1964 that
     such was the case, would you give any consideration to this
     revelation which was in no way rebutted by the company ? Ex-
     plain.

Bibliography

Davey, H. W., "The Arbitrator Speaks on Discharge and Discipline,"
    The Arbitration Journal, Vol. XVII, No. 2 (1962), pp. 97-104.

Stessin, L., Employee Discipline (Washington, D. C.: Bureau of
    National Affairs, Inc., (1960), chap. vi, "Absenteeism," pp.
    67-86; chap. vii, "Fights and Altercations," pp. 87-102; chap.
    viii, "Theft, Dishonesty, and Disloyalty," pp. 103-126; chap.
    ix, "Gambling," pp. 127-156; chap. x, "Other Violations of
    Plant Rules," pp. 136-163; chap. xi, "Incompetency," pp.
    163-199; chap. xii, "Damage to, or Loss of, Machines and
    Materials," pp. 200-210; chap. xiii, "Strikes and Strike Mis-
    conduct," pp. 211-246; chap. xiv, "Union Activity," pp. 247-
    262; chap. xv, "When Employee Resigns or Quits," pp. 263-
    279; chap. xvi, "Discipline of Supervisors," pp. 280-292; chap.
    xvii, "General Conclusions," pp. 293-310.

Stone, M., Labor-Management Contracts at Work (New York:
    Harper & Row, Publishers, 1961), chap. x, "Discharge and
    Other Forms of Discipline," pp. 191-254.

Sussman, A. M., "Work Discipline versus Private Life: An
    Analysis of Arbitration Cases," Industrial Labor Relations

Research (Cornell University), Vol. X, No. 1 (1964), pp. 3-12.

Teele, J. W., "But No Back Pay is Awarded," The Arbitration Journal, Vol. XIX, No. 2 (1964), pp. 103-112.

CHAPTER 4

Wages

The arbitrator's participation in issues over the general wage level is relatively rare. Wage level issues are crucial to the economic health of the enterprise and the living standards of the employees. The very importance of these issues to the parties underlies the extreme reluctance of either the employer or the union to entrust them to an outside third party empowered to make a final and binding determination. Thus, where existing agreements include provisions for renegotiating the general level of wages after the expiration of a given period of time—the so-called "wage reopener provisions"—it is most common to treat disputes in this area in the same manner as disputes over new contract terms, that is through the direct negotiation of the parties with the right to strike or lockout where no agreement can be attained.

Even on the rare occasions when the parties agree to submit issues over the general wage level to the arbitration process, the character of the process often resembles mediation, barring only the issue of a binding award. The arbitrator, himself, is carefully chosen for his sensitivity to the respective needs of the parties and his judgment in developing a settlement that both sides can accept and live with. The arbitrator may be encouraged to enter into private conferences with each party in order to receive a candid appraisal of its problems. The arbitration function may be centered in a board of arbitrators so that both company and union representatives may have greater participation in the decision making and thereby head off an unacceptable award. Company and union representatives may also be used by the impartial representative of the board to help gain acceptance from their respective constituents. The decision-making powers of the board may be further restricted through criteria agreed upon by the parties or through creation of limits within which the board must render its award.

The reluctance of the parties to engage in the arbitration of wage issues sometimes extends to grievances over whether the negotiated rates in the agreement have been maintained. Some agreements exclude grievances involving wage matters in whole or in part from arbitration as the terminal step in the grievance procedure. Thus, even where the issue is one of violation of the existing agreement, some contracts exclude alleged wage violations from consideration by the arbitrator. In certain agreements where such issues are specifically excluded from arbitration, the parties provide that if these issues are unsettled in the earlier steps of the grievance procedure, the union may properly authorize strike action over them. Other agreements, however, though excepting these issues from arbitral review do not except them from the general no-strike provisions of the agreement.

Where, however, the grievance procedure includes arbitration of wage matters, the arbitrator is normally concerned with whether the rates negotiated in the agreement have been properly maintained. In an era of rapidly changing job content, this is not always an easy task. In instances where the parties have bargained wage rates for specific classifications of employees presumably on the principle that higher skills and responsibilities merit higher wage rates, have these wage rates bargained by the parties been maintained for a given classification if the elements of the job have undergone change? In attempting to resolve such an issue the arbitrator must determine subsidiary facts. Has there, in effect, been a change in the job? Has such a change, in fact, increased the duties, skills, and responsibilities of the job? What is such an increase worth in dollar terms in order to maintain the wage rate intended by the parties to reflect a given admixture of skill, effort, and responsibility?

Similar problems exist when incentive rates have been bargained, for here the parties have agreed to pay wages related to the specific output of the worker. Changes in the manner of work performance bring about, on the one hand, management attempts to reduce the incentive rate where such changes tend to increase the productivity of the employee; on the other hand, changes in the work environment that tend to increase the difficulty of work performance occasion union demands for rate increases. The arbitrator again must determine subsidiary facts. Has the job changed? Has the change, in fact, affected the rate at which the worker can produce? By what degree? The latter question is so frequently enmeshed in the complicated technology of work measurement that technical arbitrators experienced in time study methods are frequently employed for this type of issue.

Other interesting questions arise over whether the contractually bargained wages have been maintained, particularly in the area of bonus payments, when for instance an employer unilaterally announces it is no longer in effect. Was the bonus a gratuity removable at the will of the employer, or had it become so integrated in the wage structure that it must be continued for the life of the agreement except through specific negotiation?

Where contracts contain wage re-opening provisions for certain groups of employees, or perhaps all of the employees in the collective bargaining unit, questions of interpretation sometimes arise over the meaning of these clauses. When may the union reopen the agreement, or phrased differently, what is the duration of the existing wage bargain? What procedures must the union follow if it desires to reopen the agreement and attempts to negotiate wage adjustments?

In recent years, there has been a tendency to negotiate a "wage package" which includes not only direct wages but other so-called fringe items such as paid holidays, vacation benefits, premium payments for overtime, and the like. Only the problems in direct wages and bonuses will be dealt with in this section of the casebook, because many of the indirect payments raise special and unique problems which can be more effectively dealt with by separate consideration.

CASES

9. The Waterville Company Case

BACKGROUND OF THE CASE

The company manufactures heavy industrial machinery at three plants located in Pittsburgh, Pennsylvania, Cleveland, Ohio, and Wheeling, West Virginia. Within the past two years the company established a job evaluation system in all three plants, and job descriptions were developed for all production jobs in each of the plants. The resulting labor grades to which the vast majority of jobs were assigned were agreed to between the company and the union and made a part of the present collective bargaining agreement. In a few instances, the tentative nature of work assignments gave rise to jobs which were evaluated on a temporary basis only with the parties' agreement that they would discuss these at a later date.

One such temporary evaluation of labor grade nine was developed for the job of tool repairman, job number twenty-five, at the Pittsburgh plant. The parties agreed that this job should be compared with those of project development tool and die maker, job number five, labor grade eleven, and die cast tool and die maker, job number fifteen, labor grade ten in order to determine its proper slotting in the labor grade scale, but cannot agree on the proper slotting. The company claims that the job should be classified in labor grade eight, whereas the union contends the job should be classified in labor grade ten.

APPLICABLE CONTRACT PROVISIONS

Section 36—Job Classifications

    (c) Jobs shall be slotted in their proper Labor Grades consistent with the classification and/or Labor Grade of the majority of like, similar, and comparable jobs in the plant listing.

(d) If the parties are unable to reach a satisfactory agreement regarding the slotting of new jobs or temporarily slotted existing jobs, then the matter shall be submitted to arbitration.

Relevant Job Descriptions

Job #5—Project Development Tool and Die Maker

Primary Function: To construct tools, dies, fixtures, machine parts, and gauges from ideas, suggestions, and conceptions furnished them by the Production Department. Occasionally work from blueprints furnished by the Engineering Department. Make their own cutting tools. Set up and operate various machine tools and equipment. Make adjustments in dies to satisfy the requirements of the Production Department. Engaged mostly in the creation and construction of complicated tools, dies, and equipment. Exercise some supervision of those who assist them and assist in training such personnel.

Experience: The successful completion of a five-year apprenticeship program.

Education: Knowledge of algebra and calculus.

Working Conditions: On occasions work station may be crowded.

Hazards: Practically none except in the normal operation of equipment where it is no greater than that of any other Machine Operator.

Safety of Others: Very little responsibility for other workmen.

Job #15—Die Cast Tool and Die Maker

Primary Function: To construct tools, dies, fixtures, machine parts, and gauges for production, working mostly from blueprints, sketches, and occasionally on oral instructions on less complicated items. Grinds own tools and occasionally constructs some simple tools.

Set up and operate various machine tools and equipment.
Makes adjustments in less complicated dies to satisfy
the requirements of the Production Department. Exercises some supervision of those who assist them and
assists in training such personnel.

Experience: Four years of training and experience.

Education: Knowledge of algebra.

Working Conditions: On occasions work station may be
crowded.

Hazards: Practically none except in the normal operation
of equipment, where it is no greater than that of any other
Machine Operator.

Job #25—Tool and Die Repairman

Primary Function: To maintain, repair, and rework tools
and dies for the Production Department. May construct
very simple tools on occasions. Set up and operate various machine tools and equipment. Exercises no supervision and engages in no training activities.

Experience: Two years of training and experience.

Education: High school education.

Working Conditions: Frequently works with poor lighting
when repairing a part on a machine set up. Encounters
dirt and considerable grease in doing repair and disas-
sembly work.

Hazards: On occasions is required to make servicing
repairs to equipment.

POSITION OF THE UNION

The work performed by the tool repairman is comparable to
that of the die cast tool and die maker. The only real difference
in the job descriptions between tool repairman, die cast tool and
die maker, and project development tool and die maker is the
degree of experience required. The company's assessment that
only two years' experience is necessary to carry out this work is

unduly low since the normal experience required in industry for
comparable jobs is four years.

Originally all construction and repair of tools and dies was
carried out by one classification. After the work was split into
several classifications, many of the employees in the lower classifications were capable of performing the higher rated work of project development tool and die maker. The tool repairman uses the
same equipment, repairs the same dies, hardens the same materials
as do employees in the other two job classifications. Because of the
diversification of duties the tool repairman must possess even greater
knowledge than that possessed by the project development tool and die
maker. On occasion, it should be noted that the die cast tool and die
maker also performs tool and die repair work.

During the establishment of the job evaluation system, the consultant employed by the company, Mr. J. R. Smith, after reviewing
the evaluation of all jobs at the three plants, concluded that the classification of tool repairman at the Pittsburgh plant was entitled to a
higher rating than the same classification in the other two plants.

POSITION OF THE COMPANY

Both the project development tool and die maker and the die cast
tool and die maker are required to construct tools and dies, whereas
the tool repairman is only required to maintain, repair, and rework
tools and dies which have been constructed. Obviously the former
jobs require more vision and creativity. They require construction
of dies from nothing more than an idea or rough sketch as well as
from blueprints, whereas the tool repairman merely has to repair
or rework parts. Even where extensive rework is necessary, he
has the physical parts on hand which he merely has to duplicate.
The die cast tool and die maker is often required to assist the project development tool and die maker, whereas the tool repairman is
not required to do so. Further, the experience necessary to carry
out the latter duties is significantly shorter and the educational requirements are considerably less.

The essential principle of job evaluation is that jobs be rated
on the requirements of those jobs rather than on the basis of the
additional skills possessed by employees who occupy those jobs.
Job evaluation rates jobs not employees. Were the tool repairman
deemed a labor grade ten job, an inequity would be created with

respect to the requirements of the project development tool and die maker and the die cast tool and die maker. This would in turn result in grievances filed by employees occupying the latter classification claiming the need for an increase in their job rating so that the proper relationship between jobs would be maintained.

The statement of consultant J. R. Smith is irrelevant to the instant issue since it is based on the relationship of the tool repairman's job in the Pittsburgh plant to that job in the other plants. The agreement requires, however, that the relationship be consistent on an intraplant rather than an interplant basis. This, of course, means the proper relationship to the job of project development tool and die maker and die cast tool and die maker classifications upon which the parties are in agreement both as to their evaluation and their relevance to the job at issue.

Suggested Discussion Questions

(a) To what extent, if any, should the statement of consultant J. R. Smith be given consideration in the determination of this case? Would it make any difference if the union had demonstrated that jobs five, fifteen, and twenty-five in the Cleveland and Wheeling plants were identical with the same jobs in the Pittsburgh plant?

(b) Is there a valid distinction between "constructing" new tools and dies and "repairing" them?

(c) What effect would the difference in working conditions and hazards have upon your determination of this case?

(d) What essential role do job descriptions play in the arbitration process in the evaluation of jobs?

10. The Ulster Company Case

BACKGROUND OF THE CASE

On October 3, 1961 the company and the union entered into a supplemental agreement to the agreement between the parties dated

July 1, 1960. Among the amendments and modifications stated
therein was the following provision:

> The Union shall have the privilege on October 1, 1962 to
> reopen this Agreement solely for the purpose of discussing
> the rate of basic per hour wages for those employees who
> work on the operation of the Herman Pneumatic Machine.
> In the event no agreement can be reached on this matter
> then either party shall have the right to cease operations.

Accordingly, on November 27, 1962 the parties entered into a
supplemental agreement "for the purpose of establishing the wage
rates and training period for the classifications of Operator and
Iron Pourer on the Herman Rol-O-Cast Pipe Machine" (Herman
Pneumatic Machine). This agreement spelled out the incremental
wage increases to be applied to those classifications over a period
from November 6, 1962 through June, 1964.

The final paragraph of that supplemental agreement states:

> In formulating this Agreement it is recognized that the
> provisions herein extend beyond the term of our present
> Agreement. It is therefore agreed that the classifications
> of Operator and Iron Pourer be excluded from any consid-
> eration affecting pay whatsoever in any Agreement nego-
> tiated in 1963. It is further agreed that this Agreement
> shall not be subject to renegotiation until April 1, 1965.
> This Agreement shall be considered as a supplement to the
> agreement dated July 1, 1960.

In a letter to the company dated April 12, 1965 the union attempted to open negotiations on the wage rates of operators and
iron pourers. In letters dated April 19, 1965 and May 5, 1965 the
company asserted that the union's failure to notify the company in
writing "at least 60 days before expiration," in effect, continued
the supplemental agreement in force for another year under the
terms of the agreement of July 1, 1960 of which the supplement
was a part.

The agreement of July 1, 1960 and the successive agreements
of October 3, 1961 and December 1, 1963 contain identical language
with respect to the duration of the respective agreements. This
language provides:

> This agreement to become effective . . . and to remain
> in full force and effect through . . . and from year to

year thereafter unless one party or the other gives notice
in writing to the opposite party at least sixty (60) days
prior to the expiration of the Agreement that it proposes
certain changes therein. If a new agreement cannot be
reached within thirty (30) days time, the existing Agreement shall automatically be extended for a period of not
more than an additional thirty (30) days, during which,
negotiations shall continue before the Federal Mediation
and Conciliation Service.

(b)   Conferences shall be held during the sixty (60) day
period, and in the event no agreement can be reached
between the parties, then either party shall have the
right to cease operations.

Not satisfied with the company's interpretation of the agreement
of July 1, 1960 (and its successor agreements), the union filed a
demand for arbitration.

POSITION OF THE UNION

The November, 1962 supplemental agreement on wage rates for
iron pourers and operators does not contain an expiration date nor
an automatic renewal of the agreement. The language is substantially
different from that of the agreement of July 1, 1960 which does provide for both a sixty-day notice of proposed changes and automatic
renewal where such notice is not given. The November, 1962 supplemental agreement provides that the wage rates negotiated therein
will not be subject to renegotiation until April 1, 1965 and provides
no further restrictions. On April 1, 1965, or at any time thereafter,
the union may without notice open negotiations on this narrow issue
of wages for operators and iron pourers. The supplemental agreement makes clear that in return for the wage increments provided
therein, the union gave up the right to seek further gains in the 1963
negotiations for these specific classifications. But clearly, it gave
up the right to renegotiate the wages contained therein only to April
1, 1965. This obviously implies that these wages are renegotiable
after that date without notice or without automatic renewal.

No basis exists for reading into the November, 1962 supplemental agreement a provision for notice or one for automatic renewal. The parties obviously knew how to write such a provision

since one has been contained in the agreement itself since 1960. Failure to include it in the supplemental agreement can only mean that the parties did not intend to subject the renegotiation of the wages of iron pourers and operators to any such restriction.

The company should have begun renegotiation of the 1962 supplemental agreement upon receipt of the union's letter of April 2, 1965, but it improperly refused to do so. An award ordering the company to renegotiate this proposal after an elapse of over four months is not a sufficient remedy. The union, therefore, requests that the arbitrator direct the parties to begin renegotiation of the 1962 supplemental agreement and further direct that the terms agreed upon be made retroactive to either April 12, 1965, or any other date he deems appropriate.

POSITION OF THE COMPANY

The November, 1962 supplemental agreement provided that it was to be made part of the Agreement of July 1, 1960. This was clearly stated, to wit:

This Agreement shall be considered as a supplement to the Agreement dated July 1, 1960.

In the 1960 agreement, as well as its successor agreements of 1961 and 1963, there was provided a sixty-day notice clause for renegotiation and an automatic renewal provision if such notice was not given. If the supplemental agreement of November, 1962 was made a part of the 1960 agreement, then all of the terms applicable to the latter agreement must be observed, including the notice and automatic renewal provisions. The union cannot make certain provisions applicable and ignore the balance of the provisions arbitrarily. The mere fact that the November, 1962 supplemental agreement is not subject to renegotiation until a certain date does not relieve the union from giving notice in accordance with the agreement provisions of which it is a supplement.

Suggested Discussion Questions

(a) Conceivably the union might have an alternate remedy by filing a refusal to bargain complaint against the company before the

National Labor Relations Board. What are the advantages and
disadvantages of such a proceeding?

(b) Should the fact that the union may have an alternative route for
redress deter the arbitrator from considering the issue under
the grievance procedure?

(c) To what extent, if at all, should the arbitrator be guided by
National Labor Relations Board policies with respect to the
requirement for notice?

(d) If, as the company points out, all other provisions of the regular
agreement are controlling, how can it be argued that the notice
and renewal provisions are an exception?

(e) Suppose that the arbitrator is impressed with the union position,
what grounds are there for rejecting the remedy which the union
seeks?

11. The Victoria Company Case

BACKGROUND OF THE CASE

For a period of at least nineteen years prior to 1964, and
possibly for a longer period of time, the company has paid an
annual Christmas bonus. The amount of this bonus followed no
fixed formula, the total amount allocated for distribution being
solely determined by the Hartman brothers, who are president and
vice president of the company, without consultation with other
company management. The distribution of the bonus amount varied
in particular cases, although essentially it was based on an employee's proportionate earnings.

In July of 1964 the union won representation rights for the production and maintenance employees of the company. An agreement
was signed on October 26, 1964 with the wage provisions made retroactive to September 9, 1964. During the early stages of negotiations
the union presented the following proposal:

Article XXIII—Past Practices

80. It is agreed that employee benefits and working
conditions presently in effect and not covered by this

Agreement shall not be eliminated nor changed except by
mutual agreement. In no case, however, shall past
practices and working conditions be effective to deprive
any employee of rights provided for him under the Agreement.

This proposal was maintained until late in the negotiations when it
was dropped allegedly when the parties agreed upon improved health,
death, and jury benefits, as well as upon a wage increase.

The company distributed a Christmas bonus in 1964 to all employees outside the bargaining unit including executives, salesmen,
supervisors, office and clerical employees, but did not distribute
any Christmas bonus to employees within the bargaining unit.

The union grieved the failure of the company to pay a Christmas
bonus to bargaining unit employees, and unable to resolve the grievance to its satisfaction, the union requested arbitration of the dispute. The parties agreed upon the following stipulation of the issue:

Is the company obligated to pay a Christmas bonus? If
so, what should the remedy be?

POSITION OF THE UNION

Since the company has admittedly paid a Christmas bonus for
over nineteen years, such a bonus has become integrated into the
wage structure regardless of changes in wages and benefits which
became effective with the initial collective bargaining agreement.
Prior to the union's winning collective bargaining rights, Plant
Superintendent Middleton addressed employees in the foundry and
machine shop and pointed out the benefits that the employees then
enjoyed as nonunion employees. Among these he listed the Christmas bonus. There were no negotiations on terminating this bonus,
and the company may not take such action unilaterally.

The company's figures on the amount of benefits gained by the
union during 1964 must be discounted. The 1964 agreement is for
two years, and the direct wage benefits over the two-year period
amount to only fifteen cents. In return the employees gave up certain incentive wage rates, a factor that may prove detrimental to
employee earnings in the long run. Moreover, the initial contract
represented a catching-up process, for the wages and benefits paid
by the Victoria Company were less than those paid by comparable

organized plants. In return for these benefits, the employees did
not knowingly surrender their rights to a Christmas bonus.

The fact that the wage provisions were made retroactive is im-
material to the instant issue. The period of retroactivity was
relatively short; wages could have been made retroactive to the date
of the election.

The mere fact that the amount of bonus depended upon the subjective judgment of the president and vice president of the company
does not convert it into a gratuity, particularly in the light of the
long history of its payment.

To read into the failure of the union to incorporate paragraph
80 of the union proposal into the negotiated agreement a presumption
that all benefits could be cut off is an unsound argument and an unsound conclusion. This is particularly true in the light of the fact
that when the union specifically asked the company if it was going
to pay the Christmas bonus, the company replied that it would take
that question up later. Many employees are afraid of a past practice
clause, and it is a difficult provision to achieve in an initial contract.

POSITION OF THE COMPANY

Although the company has distributed a Christmas bonus for a
number of years, the total amount allocated by the company as well
as the amount received by an individual employee has been extremely
variable. There is no pattern or formula upon which an individual
employee could rely from year to year. Whether a bonus was to be
given and the amount of the bonus depended entirely upon the decision
of President Hartman and his brother who is vice president in charge
of sales. No production manager, superintendent, or other managerial employee of the company has ever entered into that determination.

In all previous years employees of the company received wage
increases far below those obtained in 1964. While there were
several isolated exceptions, the average wage increase has amounted
to approximately six cents per hour per year. This is far below the
company's calculation of wage and fringe increases for 1964 totaling
nineteen cents per hour. Over and above these benefits the company
agreed as a result of 1964 negotiations to reclassify jobs in February,
1965, an obligation which the company estimates will cost an additional thirteen and one-half cents per hour. One particular benefit

which the company wishes to emphasize is that of retroactivity on
the wage increase granted in October, 1964. The cost of retroactivity alone was in excess of $9,300 and was granted under the
impression that paragraph 80 of the union's proposals had been
abandoned. The company places the total cost of the 1964 agreement at thirty-two and one-half cents per hour for the first contract
year, and thirty-five cents per hour over the two-year term.

There is no Christmas bonus provision in the agreement and no
contractual commitment to maintain conditions or benefits, although
the union had demanded such a provision during negotiations. Indeed,
the proposal demanded by the union contained a clause using the term
"benefits." The term can mean only one thing. This clause was
demanded at the outset of lengthy negotiations, repeatedly denied by
the company, and finally abandoned by the union after it had gained
other substantial benefits. This collective bargaining history is not
based on hearsay or contested versions of negotiation, but on the
written evidence and undisputed language of paragraph 80 of the
union's proposal. There is no valid answer to the company argument that a clear demand by the union for a continuation of benefits
in effect at the beginning of the negotiations had been abandoned
during the negotiations.

Although salaried employees including executives, office, sales,
and technical employees received a Christmas bonue, they did not
share in the gains received by union employees within the bargaining
unit. Salaried employees did not receive a general increase during
1964, although some did receive merit increases. There was no
thought of impairing the union position in this move. The company
merely faced a different picture than it had ever faced before.

Suggested Discussion Questions

(a) One of the issues raised in the instant case is under what conditions do bonuses become so integrated or "locked in" the wage
rate structure that they may not be removed except by specific
agreement. What criteria might be used to determine this issue
in the case of Christmas bonuses?

(b) In what respect are bonuses different from other conditions of
employment, say for instance a coffee break, with respect to
the unilateral exercise of management rights?

(c) Of what relevance is the amount of the wage settlement gained
     by the union? For what purpose do you think the company intro-
     duced this information?

(d) Do the facts that the negotiations were the first for the parties
     and that the agreement represents an initial contract influence
     your opinion in any way? Explain.

(e) Is the bargaining history more favorable to the company or to
     the union claim? Explain.

12. The Tatem Company Case

BACKGROUND OF THE CASE

The company is engaged in general foundry work. Formerly it
operated two plants, the Barrington plant which during an early
period was not organized, and the Springfield plant which was organized. The former plant was principally engaged in the production
of fittings.

A fitting is produced by two methods, generally described as a
Northern method and a Southern method. Although the total costs
of the methods are about equal, the production per day and production
per square foot of space is much greater under the Southern method.
Piece rates under the Southern method are also considerably lower.

Prior to its organization by a union, the Barrington plant was
converted from the Northern to the Southern method. When the
methods were changed, the piece rates were arbitrarily and un-
evenly reduced, admittedly "without rhyme or reason." An across-
the-board reduction in rates was made during February and March
of 1962 which did not remove the inequities, but did bring the piece
rates down to where they "straddled" the so-called Southern line of
piece-rate payments, with some rates above and others below this
line.

Shortly thereafter the Barrington plant was organized, and the
initial contract was negotiated in July, 1962. Recognition of the
chaotic piece-rate structure was evidenced by the insertion of the
following provision in the agreement:

  (h) In the event that the piece-work price for any
fitting is thought to be out of line, it is agreed that the
Company and the Union will meet for the purpose of
working out a mutually satisfactory rate.

Following the negotiation of this agreement, however, the Barrington
plant was closed down, and the molding of all fittings was transferred
to the Springfield plant.

During the transition period, the company and union held meetings
which resulted in a memorandum of agreement on molding piece-rate
prices. This agreement stated, in part:

(5) Piece-Work Prices

  It was agreed that the piece-work prices for fitting
molding operations should be those currently in effect
at Alabama Pipe Company.

The company never imposed these prices because of the wide number
of patterns in operation and the fact that it felt that the rates would
average out. In individual cases, whenever a molder would question
the piece rate he was receiving, the company would investigate, and
if the rate was below the agreed-upon rate, the company would raise
that specific rate, but it would at the same time look over all the
items he made, and where any rates were above the agreed-upon
rate, the company would unilaterally lower those items. Thus,
this procedure would gradually remove the admitted inequities and
as long as conditions remained about average, according to the
company, "nobody got hurt."

The specific dispute arose when the grievant, Mr. William
Dalton, discovered upon receiving his pay envelope that on February
9, 1965 the company had unilaterally reduced the piece-rate price
on a four-inch T fitting from forty cents to thirty-six cents. He had
produced these fittings for over a year at the forty-cent price, but
the company in the pay envelope covering the period in question had
given him forty cents for a certain amount of these fittings and
thirty-six cents for the remainder.

Mr. Dalton spoke to Company Manager Larson and was informed
that thirty-six cents was the price he would receive in the future for
that particular piece, but that since Mr. Larson had not spoken to
him about it previously, it was a "breach of ethics" and he would be
awarded the higher price up to the date of the above meeting.

The union objected to the unilateral reduction of the piece rate
and unable to resolve the dispute to its satisfaction, filed a demand
for arbitration.

APPLICABLE CONTRACT PROVISIONS

Article XII—Discounts

(g) Molders to be paid full Board prices plus percentage on, for all castings that are sold by the Company.

(h) In the event that the piece-work price for any
fitting is thought to be out of line, it is agreed that the
Company and the Union will meet for the purpose of working
out a mutually satisfactory rate.

POSITION OF THE UNION

The "board prices" referred to in Paragraph (g) of Article XII
are the prices in effect at the time the parties negotiated the agreement. The union at the time of negotiations recognized that these
piece rates were more favorable than most and as a consequence
negotiated a modest wage increase of only five cents per hour as
contrasted to the eighteen-cent increase negotiated for nonincentive
operations. Alabama or Southern board prices are not mentioned
in the agreement. There is not one "board price" nor two "board
prices," but a whole series of "board prices." The company raised
no question about Alabama prices at the time of negotiations, and it
was the intent of the union to refer to the existing piece-rate prices.

The memorandum of May, 1963 which resulted from the closing
of the Barrington plant and the transfer of operations to the Springfield plant did not pertain to the work at issue, so-called hand or
skill pattern operation. When these operations were transferred,
the company instituted a new more mechanized method known as the
"squeeze operation," and it was with respect to this latter operation
that the memorandum on piece-rate prices was directed, rather than
to the skill method utilized in the instant grievance.

In no event does the company have the unilateral right to reduce
piece rates as Paragraph (h) of Section XII makes clear. A "mutually
satisfactory rate" is one which is agreed upon, and not one unilaterally
imposed by the company. If the company lowered the piece-rate

prices of any jobs in the past, prior to the instant situation, certainly the union was never advised of such action, nor has the contract procedure been followed.

The union, therefore, requests that the company be directed to restore the reduction and make whole all employees whose earnings were affected by the company's improper action.

POSITION OF THE COMPANY

The term "Board prices" referred to in the agreement are the Alabama or Southern board prices. The company has agreed to pay these prices and has done its part to abide by those provisions of the agreement. Specific mention of Alabama board rates or Southern board rates in the agreement is unnecessary. The fact that the molding method is the Southern method makes clear to anyone with knowledge of the industry that Southern rather than Northern rates should apply.

Nor does the memorandum of agreement of May, 1963 have the restrictive intent suggested by the union. If the parties had intended a restricted meaning, they would not have used the broad language contained in that memorandum. The memorandum provides for "the piece-work prices for fitting molding operations." This language makes no distinction between hand and mechanized work.

Because of the changeover from Northern to Southern methods of operation, and because of the arbitrary method of adjusting rates prior to organization by the union, the company has been left with inequities in the piece-rate structure. Since that time the company has made a concerted effort to reduce these inequities by raising the rates on certain jobs and lowering the rates on others. Although it has normally proceeded on this program only when an employee questions a rate, the company has on numerous occasions, both prior to and after union organization of these operations, proceeded on its own motion. Many such changes have been made between 1963 and 1965.

Although the agreement provides that there should be a meeting to discuss piece-rate changes, the company does not feel that this is necessary. Any time a molder feels that there is a question about a rate to be paid for a given job, he is completely free to bring it to the company's attention, and the rate will be changed without the formality of a meeting.

(a) Considerable attention was paid by both the company and the union to the question of interpreting the term "board prices." Do you think resolution of this issue is necessary to deciding the specific matter before the arbitrator? Explain. Assuming the answer to the above question is in the negative, do you think the arbitrator should still dispose of the issue, or concentrate on only those matters necessary to his reaching a decision? Explain.

(b) Although at first blush the company's method of handling its difficulties may seem to have the virtue of simplicity and a common-sense approach, the method could be fraught with grave problems for the employees involved and the union as an institution. Explain.

(c) What facts, if any, might be introduced to indicate that the union has waived its rights under Paragraph (h) of the agreement?

(d) Suppose the grievance procedure on the above agreement provided only for disputes between the individual employee and his supervisor in the first instance, and made no provisions for so-called policy grievances. Under these conditions do you believe that the union could entertain an action in arbitration in the above circumstances if the aggrieved employee did not choose to submit a grievance? Explain.

13. The Sweetwater Company Case

BACKGROUND OF THE CASE

The Sweetwater Company is a small owner-managed producer of food products. On Election Day, November 3, 1964, approximately eight employees approached Chief Steward Brown during the morning and requested time off for voting in accordance with the collective bargaining agreement. Mr. Brown approached the owner of the company and informed him of the employees' desires, pointing out that under the provision in question the owner was free to specify

the hour at which these employees could be excused for voting purposes. The owner professed ignorance of any such provision in the
agreement and allegedly stated that the employees could vote on
their own time after work.

The owner contacted his attorney and after learning that the
agreement did in fact provide for time off for voting purposes, he
called Mr. Brown into his office and informed him that he was
closing the plant at 2:30 P. M. , one hour before the normal shift
closing, so that employees would have an extra hour for the purpose
of voting. Mr. Brown questioned the owner about paying the employees. The owner stated that "these people would be paid, " but
apparently the owner meant by that phrase the employees who had
voted, whereas Mr. Brown assumed he meant all employees who
were required to leave early.

The plant was closed down one hour early. Some employees
other than production employees, however, worked the full work
day. On the following day, the owner passed out a form requesting
voting employees to indicate that they had voted and to designate the
polling place where they had cast their ballot. The owner made clear
that only those employees who signed the form would be compensated.
On the advice of Mr. Brown, no employee signed the list, and, therefore, no employee has been paid.

The union grieved the manner in which the company treated the
voting privilege accorded by Article 11 of the agreement, and unable to resolve the issue to its satisfaction, the union filed a demand for arbitration.

APPLICABLE CONTRACT PROVISION

Article 11

Employees, if they desire, may take off one (1) hour
with pay on Election Day for the purpose of voting; said
hour to be taken off to be specified by the Employer.

POSITION OF THE UNION

Under the provisions of Article 11, "employees, if they desire,
may take time off with pay for the purpose of voting. " The provision is couched in voluntary terms and contemplates that those

voting will be excused from the plant and will return. There is
nothing in the section which indicates that it is mandatory on the
part of the employee or that a one-hour layoff on Election Day is
to be imposed upon all employees. A production shutdown is inconsistent with this language. Since there were employees who did not
choose to vote during working hours, they should have been permitted
to work and not forced to leave the plant one hour early.

The company argument that a shutdown was necessary because
key employees were going to vote is not valid. First, the owner
never attempted to ascertain this point. He was completely unaware of the number of employees who desired to leave and which
employees these were. Secondly, even assuming that there were
key people who desired to take time off to vote, the agreement contemplates that they will be given time off in such a manner as not to
interfere with production. This is why the company is given the
right under the agreement to stipulate the hour. If key people were
involved, the company had the responsibility of scheduling their
time off so as to avoid production difficulties.

The manner in which the company handled this incident could
nullify what the union bargained in the agreement. Company in-
sistence on a production shutdown for one hour on Election Day in
order to satisfy the requirements of Article 11 could become costly
to employees who were ineligible to vote or who did not desire to
vote and thus nullify the privilege bargained by the union for those
employees who desire to vote during working hours.

The company, therefore, violated the agreement when it
scheduled an early shift closing on Election Day and agreed to pay
only those employees who attested that they had voted. The union
requests that all employees on the payroll on Election Day, November
3, 1964, be awarded one hour's pay.

POSITION OF THE COMPANY

When Shop Steward Brown approached the owner of the company
about excusing employees from work in order to vote, he did not indicate the number of people who wanted time off to vote. Based upon
the fact that included in this number could be key employees, the
owner decided that the only way to handle the matter was to shut
down the plant, because if certain key employees were to take the
hour off, orderly production could not continue. For this reason,
the company shut down the plant one hour early.

Article 11 of the agreement gives the company the right to determine what hour the employee may take off for the purpose of
voting. The company merely exercised its right when it closed the
plant one hour early. The obligation of the company to pay is restricted to those people who actually voted. The obvious purpose of
the provision is to encourage the right of franchise; therefore, if
employees do not exercise their right of franchise, they forfeit that
contract benefit. The company has at all times been prepared to
pay those employees who voted and will submit their names and the
polling places at which they voted.

The manner in which the company handled the situation was not
a deliberate subversion of the provisions of Article 11. The company contends that there must be a showing of intent to subvert, if
the company is to be held in violation of that article of the agreement.

Suggested Discussion Questions

(a) Suppose the owner attempted to satisfy Article 11 by announcing
that all employees who desired to vote would be excused from
the plant at 2:30 P.M. Under these conditions is he entitled to
evidence that the employees did, in fact, vote?

(b) Under the above supposition, the owner found that 25 per cent of
his employees desired to take advantage of early leaving and
orderly production could not continue. Under these conditions
would he be within his rights to close down the plant one hour
early without reimbursing the nonvoter?

(d) The collective bargaining agreement controlling this situation
contains a nondiscrimination clause banning discrimination
against any employee because of "race, creed, color, sex,
age, or nationality." Does such a clause have any relevance
to the instant situation? Explain.

(e) Suppose the union's claim of contract violation was upheld,
how would you fashion the remedy for those few employees who
worked a full day, but nevertheless were denied the right to
vote during working hours?

Bibliography

Belcher, David W., Wage and Salary Administration, 2d ed.
(Englewood Cliffs, N. J.: Prentice-Hall, Inc., 1962), chap.
vii, "Internal Wage Structure Determination," pp. 175-198.

Bernstein, Irving, The Arbitration of Wages (Berkeley and Los
Angeles, Calif.: University of California Press, 1954), chap.
i, "Introduction," pp. 1-4; chap. ii, "Wage Arbitration: the
Institution," pp. 14-33; chap. iii, "Some Procedural Problems,"
pp. 34-50; chap. iv, "Criteria of Wage Determination: I,"
pp. 51-71; chap. v, "Criteria of Wage Determination: II,"
pp. 72-105; chap. vi, "Conclusions," pp. 106-116.

Davis, Pearce, "Incentive Problems (Workshop No. 2)—a Summary,"
Management Rights and the Arbitration Process, Proceedings
of the Ninth Annual Meeting of the National Academy of Arbitrators, Cleveland, Ohio, January 26-28, 1956 (Washington,
D. C.: Bureau of National Affairs, Inc., 1956), pp. 50-53.

Dunlop, John T. and James J. Healy, Collective Bargaining -
Principles and Cases, rev. ed. (Homewood, Ill.: Richard D.
Irwin, Inc., 1953), Part II, Section H: "General Wage Changes,"
pp. 343-391; Section I: "Wage Structure," pp. 392-432.

Justin, Jules J., "Arbitrating a Wage Dispute," The Arbitration
Journal, Vol. III, New Series no. 4 (1948), pp. 228-31.

Slichter, Sumner H., James J. Healy, and E. Robert Livernash,
The Impact of Collective Bargaining on Management (Washington,
D. C.: The Brookings Institution, 1960), chap. xvii, "Wage
Incentives," pp. 490-529; chap. xviii, "Measured Day Work,"
pp. 530-557; chap. xix, "Evaluated Rate Structures," pp.
558-591; chap. xx, "Wage Structure Considerations," pp. 591-
624.

Trotta, Maurice S., Labor Arbitration - Principles, Procedures,
and Issues (New York: Simmons-Boardman Publishing Co.,
1961), Part II: "Job Evaluation and Classification," pp. 274-
279.

CHAPTER 5

Vacations and Holidays

HOLIDAY PAY

One of the most common issues in matters of holiday pay concerns the eligibility of employees for such payment. The eligibility of employees for holiday pay is, in part, determined through deciding which of two contrasting philosophies underlie its payment. The original concept of holiday pay was to prevent a loss of income to the employee who otherwise would have worked on that day had it not been for the occurrence of the holiday. Under this philosophy the agreement language makes clear that only those employees who otherwise would have worked are eligible for such payments; holiday pay is not given for holidays falling during vacation periods, layoff periods, or during periods of extended illness or injury.

A later concept of holiday pay emerged as a fringe benefit paid employees in lieu of increased hourly earnings under so-called "package settlements." Under this philosophy the parties to an agreement have the alternative of bargaining higher hourly rates or of bargaining an increase in the number of holidays in the determination of the "total wage package" to be mutually agreed upon. Viewed in this light, holiday pay comes out of the annual earnings of all employees, whether or not they happen to work on the day in question. The eligibility for such pay accrues by reason of prior employment and the meeting of specified requirements in the agreement. The question of which of these philosophies should prevail is completely a matter of negotiation between the parties, and the intention of the parties in this regard may be determined by an examination of the agreement language, bargaining history, and/or past practice in the interpretation of the agreement.

Where contracts provide for holiday provisions of the "fringe benefit" rather than "monetary loss" variety, specific requirements for eligibility are, nevertheless, commonly spelled out in the agreement. One of the most common of these is the so-called "surrounding day" requirement which provides that an employee must work on certain days surrounding the holiday. The primary purpose of this requirement is to discourage employee absenteeism or the "stretching" of holiday periods. Depending on how this provision is phrased, however, it may deny eligibility to those who are absent from work through no fault of their own.

VACATION PAY

Although a few vacation plans of the "monetary loss" variety still exist, as when a plant closes down for a stated period of weeks during the summer months and employees are granted a proportion of this loss of income in proportion to their length of service, the overwhelming majority of vacation plans are of the "fringe benefit" variety. The usual question before the arbitrator in disputes over vacations, as in holiday pay issues, is whether the employee was eligible for a vacation, and, if so, for how much vacation.

The problem in determining vacation eligibility, however, is much more complex than for holidays. Several reasons underlie this. First, varying vacation amounts are provided for employees with varying lengths of service. Secondly, employees accumulate service credits at different times of the year, depending on the particular day on which they started employment. Thirdly, unlike holidays, vacations may usually be taken at the employee's convenience over a relatively broad spectrum of the calendar year.

Where an employee's eligibility date is synonymous with his anniversary date, administrative problems may result because eligibility dates differ for each employee. To avoid these complexities some agreements set an arbitrary eligibility date, say June 1, against which the service credits of each employee are matched in order to determine the amount of vacation due. In either of these situations, the problem for the arbitrator is one of attempting to discover from the frequently complicated contract terminology what the parties really intended.

A further complication is the right of laid-off employees to vacation benefits. Where the contract has no express provision covering this, the intent of the parties must be gleaned from the contract procedures covering eligibility. Even where agreements seem on the surface to be rather specific in prorating vacations under conditions of partial work during the vacation year, the application of the prorating plans may become quite complex in terms of varying eligibility dates of the work force. Under many ageements it is a far from easy matter to determine under all conditions the amount of vacation for which a given employee is eligible.

CASES

14. The Newmark Company Case

BACKGROUND OF THE CASE

The grievant, Miss Ann Connors, retired voluntarily in accordance with the company's pension plan on August 31, 1963. This day, a Friday, was her last working day. The following Monday, September 3, 1962, was Labor Day and was observed by the company as a paid holiday. The company denied the grievant holiday pay on the grounds she was an annuitant. Unable to resolve the matter to its satisfaction, the union filed a demand for arbitration.

APPLICABLE CONTRACT PROVISIONS

<u>Section XI—Holidays and Vacations</u>

1. Holidays

     a. Holidays observed by the Company will be New Year's Day, Washington's Birthday, Good Friday, Memorial Day, Independence Day, Labor Day, Thanksgiving, and Christmas.

     e. Employees will be paid for such holidays at their average earned rate.

     f. The above payment will be made only to hourly paid employees who are on the active roll on the last working day before the observed holiday, and who earned some wages during the week in which such holiday falls or any of the four preceding weeks, provided that employees who are separated at any time during December 31 in any year shall not be entitled to holiday pay for New Year's Day in the following year.

Section XIV-A—Arbitration

D. Notwithstanding any other provisions of this Agreement, no arbitrator shall, without specific written agreement of the Company and the Union with respect to the arbitration proceeding before him, be authorized to:

    (1) Add to, detract from, or in any way alter the provisions of this Agreement or any Supplement or local supplement to this Agreement;

    (4) Make any award involving any matter relating to any pension and/or insurance agreement between the parties, any pension or insurance plan referred to or made a part of any such agreement, or the establishment, change, interpretation, application, or administration of any pension or insurance plan; . . .

POSITION OF THE COMPANY

The long-established, uncontested practice of the company has been to preclude holiday pay to annuitants. No annuitant has ever been granted holiday payment for a holiday occurring after his transfer from the active to the annuity rolls. The union has never, until the present instance, protested such nonpayment. Nor did it submit grievances on behalf of three other employees who retired under identical circumstances on the same date as the grievant.

The negotiation history of the clause in question makes clear that its unusual language was meant to cover a union complaint against local management laying off employees several days before a holiday in order to avoid holiday payment to them. Any change in liberalizing the language in the 1957 negotiations could only have pertained to laid-off employees.

To pay an individual holiday pay for a period during which he is already receiving other benefits, namely pension benefits, is improper. Annuitants are not employees in an active, contractual sense and, therefore, do not qualify as "employees" within the meaning of Section XI, 1 (f) of the agreement. It should be noted that the pension and insurance agreement provides that retirement benefits will not be paid for any month during which wages are received from the company.

POSITION OF THE UNION

The provisions of Section XI, 1 (f) of the agreement are clear
and unambiguous. The grievant was on the active payroll on the
last working day before the observed holiday and earned wages during
the four preceding weeks. Therefore, under the clear terms of the
agreement the grievant is eligible for holiday pay.

Past practice cannot alter clear contract language. Further,
even where contract language is ambiguous, the practice must be
clear, undeviating, and at least impliedly agreed upon by the parties.
Only two prior cases were introduced by the company; certainly this
does not evidence a practice or precedent. To support the company
would circumvent the expressed language with respect to holiday pay
in the agreement. The arbitrator is expressly prohibited from doing
this under Section XIV-A of the agreement. If the company desires
a clear-cut option on this matter, it should negotiate such an option
with the union.

Negotiation history does not support the company's position.
The union points to the specific exception made to the granting of
holiday pay for New Year's Day to those separated on December 31.
This proves the union's contention with respect to those separated
immediately prior to other holidays. The company's interpretation
that the clause was meant to include holiday pay for only those laid
off from lack of work is absurd. The negotiators of the agreement
were not tyros, but individuals of long experience in negotiating
contract language. If the parties had intended that only those parties
laid off for lack of work were to receive holiday pay, it would have
been simple to so state in the agreement.

Merely because the grievant is granted a benefit under the pension system, she is not precluded from receiving a holiday benefit
contained in the agreement. When an employee is placed on a payroll other than the active payroll, he still retains any benefit ac-
crued contractually prior to his removal from the active roll. The
dispute before the arbitrator involves only the interpretation and
application of the holiday provision in the agreement. Nor can he
be influenced by the nature of specific provisions in the pension and
insurance agreement, since the interpretation of these provisions
is beyond the scope of his authority under the provisions of Section
D (4) of Article XIV-A of the agreement.

(a) Would you consider negotiation history or past practice a better
indication of the parties' intent in the interpretation of an ambiguous contract clause? To what extent, if any, do you believe
that either past practice or negotiation history should serve to
modify clear contract language?

(b) Where provisions in a collective bargaining agreement seemingly
conflict, a sound rule of contract interpretation is to interpret
the provisions in such fashion as to reduce or minimize any conflict. Should this rule be utilized in the instant situation to resolve the conflict between the labor agreement and the pension
and insurance agreement where the arbitrator is forbidden by
contract from interpreting the rules of the pension and insurance
agreement?

(c) Would the fact that the grievant became an annuitant rather than
a laid-off employee affect your answer in the instant situation?
Suppose the action giving rise to the grievance was a voluntary
quit; would this change your answer?

15. The Oregon Company Case

BACKGROUND OF THE CASE

On November 9, 1962, Mrs. Theresa Warren requested and
received a leave of absence from the company for the period from
November 20, 1962 to December 2, 1962 for the purpose of taking
care of the children of her daughter-in-law during the latter's con-
finement. Upon her return to work, Mrs. Warren discovered that
she was not awarded holiday pay for Thursday, November 22 and
Friday, November 23, the Thanksgiving holiday for which other employees were awarded holiday pay. Mrs. Warren grieved the action
and upon denial of her grievance by the company, the union requested
arbitration of the grievance.

APPLICABLE CONTRACT PROVISIONS

<u>Article XI—Holidays</u>

    <u>Section 2.</u> A. <u>Qualifications.</u> Holiday pay shall be paid only to employees who worked their last scheduled workday before and their first scheduled workday after the holiday unless specifically excused by the Employer from working one or both of the specified days on application of employee at least two working days prior to the holiday, or unless the employee is absent due to other legitimate causes as: vacations, jury service, death in the immediate family, personal or occupational illness or injury not in excess of three (3) months, compulsory attendance at court meetings, emergencies and other situations which develop making it necessary for the employee to take time off.

<u>Article XIII—Leaves of Absence</u>

    <u>Section 1.</u> <u>General.</u> An employee, upon written request to his Foreman or Supervisor and for reasonable cause, shall be granted a leave of absence without pay up to six months.

POSITION OF THE COMPANY

    The rights of the grievant arise under Article XIII of the agreement which governs leaves of absence. That section specifically states that leaves of absence are to be taken without pay, and such a statement includes not only hourly rates of pay but also all other benefits which arise out of the employer-employee relationship.

    The grievant cannot qualify under the provisions of Section 2-A of Article XI since she had no scheduled work day before or after the holidays in question. She was excused on a voluntary absence from the plant. Nor can she qualify under the general exception to the qualification requirements since they require an employee to be excused from working <u>on one or both of the specified days</u> surrounding the holiday. Specified <u>days</u>, the company urges, cannot be translated into weeks. She cannot further qualify under the specific listed reasons for which holiday pay would be given. The parties omitted leaves of absence from the list, which omission

indicates their intention that leaves of absence would be without pay.
If the parties had intended to award holiday pay to those employees
on leaves of absence, it would have been inserted in the cited exceptions.

The situation of employee Ann George cited by the union can be
distinguished from the instant situation by the fact that she returned
to work on the day following the holiday for which she was awarded
holiday pay. Moreover, one incident does not create a practice. On
the contrary, in the case of employee Gertrude Hoover, who secured
a three months' leave of absence to vacation in Europe, the company
denied holiday pay for two intervening holidays without complaint or
grievance from the union.

POSITION OF THE UNION

The grievant manifestly qualifies for the two holidays in question
in at least three ways. First, she worked her last scheduled work-
day before her leave of absence and the first scheduled work day after
her leave of absence. Therefore, she qualifies under the qualifi-
cation section itself. Secondly, after setting up qualifications, the
agreement proceeds to set up exceptions from the qualifying language. One general exception states:

Unless specifically excused by the Employer from working
one or both of the specified days on application of the employee at least two working days prior to the holiday . . .

Since Mrs. Warren was specifically excused by the company for the
period of her leave of absence, that is, from November 20, 1962 to
December 2, 1962, she also qualifies for holiday pay under the
general exception. Finally, Mrs. Warren is entitled to holiday pay
under the last listed exception which reads:

Emergencies and other situations which develop making
it necessary for the employee to take time off.

A careful reading of the exceptions reveals that there was no intent
to exclude exceptions other than those listed. The union points to
the word "as" in the language "due to other legitimate causes as
. . . " This language, the union urges, shows an intent to illustrate exceptions rather than to limit them. Thus, the intent of the
parties was to prevent the unauthorized stretching of holidays,

rather than excluding from holiday pay the employee who was authorized to take time off from the plant.

Article XIII which provides for leaves of absence without pay
refers to the daily wages and not to the various additional emoluments
and/or benefits to which the employee is entitled. The union points
to the fact that under the agreement the employee on leave of absence
still receives the company contribution to his insurance benefit. The
reason that leaves of absence are not specified as such in Section
2-A of the agreement is that they are included in the general exception "unless specifically excused" and in the last specified exception, "emergencies and other situations which develop making
it necessary for the employee to take time off." These exceptions
clearly cover leaves of absence.

In addition to contract language, past practice supports the
union's interpretation of the agreement. Employee Ann George was
on a leave of absence from March 30, 1960 to April 18, 1960 because of the illness of her mother-in-law. When she returned, she
was denied holiday pay for Good Friday. Mrs. George filed a
grievance which the company settled by awarding her holiday pay.
Employee Catherine Brown requested the company to expand the
Memorial Day holiday in 1963 (May 30 and May 31) into a five-day
holiday by asking for Monday, June 3, as a day off. She received
approval for the request and was awarded holiday pay. Both of
these incidents took place under the identical contract language
which applies to the instant situation. The case of employee
Gertrude Hoover in which the company denied holiday pay without
grievance by the union can be distinguished on the grounds that the
employee took the leave for a vacation in Europe and that before the
leave was officially granted, the company cleared beforehand with
the union its unwillingness to give holiday pay for holidays occurring
within a three-month vacation leave.

Suggested Discussion Questions

(a) Does the language of the agreement indicate that the parties in-
    tended to bargain a clause of the "fringe benefit" or the "mone-
    tary loss" variety? Explain clearly.

(b) The union offers alternative pleading in its contention that the
    grievant qualified in three different methods under the pro-

visions of Section 2-A of the agreement. Which of these three do you consider most relevant to the facts of this specific case? Indicate why you believe the others to be less relevant.

(c) Of the two incidents mentioned by the union (the George and Brown incidents), which do you consider to be the more relevant? Indicate the basis for your conclusion.

(d) In what way is the language of Section 2-A of the agreement internally inconsistent? How would you, as an arbitrator, interpret the language to remove the inconsistency?

16. The Maxwell Corporation Case

BACKGROUND OF THE CASE

Four employees of the company were on layoff status during the Independence Day holiday in 1962. The specific period of layoff differed for each employee according to the following schedule:

Employee	Last Day Worked Before Holiday	First Day Worked After Holiday
Patrick Maxwell	6/28/62	8/ 2/62
Leroy Nunn	6/11/62	8/ 8/62
Alvin Oates	6/24/62	8/24/62
Eugene Parr	7/ 2/62	8/ 1/62

The last day worked before the holiday for each employee was the last scheduled work day for that employee and the first day worked after the holiday by each employee was the first scheduled work day for that employee. The plant, however, worked steadily throughout the interim that the employees were on layoff.

In lieu of presenting arguments at a scheduled hearing, the parties agreed to waive all position statements and mailed to the arbitrator the brief statement of facts enumerated above along with a copy of their current agreement. The parties requested the arbitrator to present a written award and opinion upholding or rejecting the claim of the listed employees for holiday pay for Independence Day, 1962.

APPLICABLE CONTRACT PROVISIONS

Article VI—Holidays

Section 1. The following shall be recognized as holidays under the terms of this Agreement: Christmas Day, New Year's Day, Memorial Day, Fourth of July, Labor Day, and Thanksgiving Day.

Section 2. Employees shall be paid at their average hourly rate of pay for the aforementioned holidays provided they work their scheduled day before and after the holiday, unless prevented by sickness or injury from doing so. For work performed on any holiday listed herein, employees shall be paid time and one-half in addition to holiday pay.

Section 3. In the event one of the above enumerated holidays should occur during the annual vacation period, employees shall be paid for the holiday in addition to their vacation pay.

Suggested Discussion Questions

(a) What are the advantages and disadvantages of the arbitration procedure invoked by the company and the union in this case?

(b) From the skeletal facts given and the applicable contract provisions, develop a complete set of company and union contentions for the parties in the instant case.

(c) What do you consider to be the key contract language in resolving this issue?

17. The Rangeley Company Case

BACKGROUND OF THE CASE

On July 3, 1960 the company shut down for a one-week vacation period. On February 9 and 10, 1961, the company laid off forty-one employees. There was no dispute concerning the propriety of the layoff or the application of the seniority provisions of the agreement. The company paid to the laid-off employees vacation pay prorated from the anniversary date of each employee's employment. The union contended that the vacation pay should be prorated from the employee's eligibility date, that is, from the date when the employee was last eligible for vacation pay.

The union grieved the company action as follows:

> The vacation pay for the employees laid off was not figured correctly as per Section 13 of the current agreement. Some senior employees received less vacation pay than junior employees in the laid-off group.

The company submitted the following answer:

> Vacations were paid to employees laid off February 9 and 10, 1961, strictly in accordance with Section 13 of the current Labor Agreement between the Shopman's Union #606 and The Rangeley Company, except for the vacation computed for Warren Kaiser, Jr., which was in error.

Failing to reach a satisfactory adjustment of the issue, the union filed a demand for arbitration.

APPLICABLE CONTRACT PROVISIONS

Article 13—Vacations

(A) Each of the Company's employees to whom this agreement is applicable, who, in each year this agreement remains in effect, shall have been in the continuous service of the Company at least 12 months, and who shall have worked during the period establishing his or her vacation eligibility, as hereinafter set forth, the requisite and qualifying number of hours hereinafter required and set forth, shall be granted a vacation in accordance with the following schedule, with pay at the regular straight time hourly rate received by such employee at the time the vacation is taken.

Length of Employees' Continuous Service with the Company	Number of Consecutive Days (Calendar) Vacation Commencing Monday	Number of Vacation Hours Pay
1 but less than 2 years	7	40
2 but less than 3 years	8	48
3 but less than 4 years	9	56
4 but less than 5 years	10	64
5 but less than 6 years	14	80
6 but less than 7 years	15	88
7 but less than 8 years	16	96
8 but less than 9 years	17	104
9 but less than 10 years	18	112
10 years or more	21	120

(B) As a further condition of participating in the fore-going plan, employees, otherwise eligible for a vacation thereunder, and whose continuous employment with the Company is twelve (12) months or more, must have worked for the Company during the year next preceding anniversary date of employment a total of at least 1,560 clock hours.

(C) Should an employee who has acquired one or more years service with the Company fail to furnish the fore-going qualifications for vacation either as result of failure to work the qualifying number of clock hours, or as result of termination for any reason whatsoever, such employee shall receive prorated vacation pay on the basis of 1/12th of the vacation pay he or she would have been entitled to on his or her preceding and/or succeeding eligibility date for each (130) clock hours worked for the Company during the (12) month period immediately prior to his or her preceding and/or succeeding eligibility date, but not to exceed the number of hours' vacation pay such employee would have received had he or she become eligible for full vacation benefits.

POSITION OF THE UNION

Logic and equity both favor the union's position in this matter. Section 13 B of the agreement obviously applies only to employees who have qualified by working a minimum of 1,560 clock hours during the measuring period. Section 13 C applies to employees who have not acquired the requisite clock hours during the measuring period and applies particularly to those employees who are terminated for any reason. Logically applying the simple meaning of Section 13 C, the company should have computed clock hours commencing July 3, 1960 in order to determine the proper prorated vacation pay.

Fairness also dictates that the union position should prevail. When the company terminates an employee's services through no fault of his own, the agreement should be construed as liberally as possible. Further, under the method used by the company, some senior employees received less vacation allowance than junior employees.

POSITION OF THE COMPANY

Article 13 of the agreement must be considered in its entirety. It clearly provides two prerequisites for the payment of vacation pay: first, length of continuous service; secondly, a specified number of clock hours of employment. The length of service requirement stated in Section A of Article 13 obviously is defined in terms of the employee's anniversary date. The actual employment requirement contained in Section B of Article 13 is also expressly defined in terms of the employee's anniversary date. The mere fact that the language in Section C of Article 13 rather loosely refers to the term "eligibility date" without definition certainly does not and cannot have the effect of broadening the vacation rights of persons who have terminated their service with the company as compared with the rights of employees remaining at work. The only logical conclusion that can be drawn is that the eligibility date for the computation of vacation benefits whether they be full benefits or prorated benefits is the anniversary date of employment. The agreement does not define eligibility date in any other manner, and in the absence of any specific definition of the word, it must be interpreted in the context of the language used elsewhere in Article 13.

Suggested Discussion Questions

(a) Distinguish between the anniversary date of an employee and his eligibility date with regard to the determination of his vacation pay.

(b) Is there any ambiguity within the provisions of Section 13 (A),
     (B), and (C), and if so, how should this ambiguity be resolved?
     Explain.

(c) If the decision is rendered for the union, might it be possible
     for inequities to arise? Explain.

(d) What provision or provisions would you recommend that the
     parties insert in Section 13 to eliminate future disputes of
     this nature?

18. The Bangor Company Case

BACKGROUND OF THE CASE

The aggrieved employees were hired in January, 1962 and laid
off in September of that year. They were awarded three days'
vacation pay for the 1962 vacation period.

The grievants did not perform any work during the calendar
year 1963, and were not awarded vacation pay. Some employees
also laid off in September of 1962 returned to work in February of
1963 and received their 1963 vacation pay. Other employees laid
off at the same time returned to work in December of 1963 and received their vacation pay.

Failing to reach a satisfactory resolution of the issue, the union
filed a demand for arbitration claiming 1963 vacation pay for the
grievants.

APPLICABLE CONTRACT PROVISIONS

Article V—Vacations

Section 5.0

Length of Continuous Service	Days of Vacation Each Year	Hours of Pay
6 months but less than 1 year	3	24
1 year but less than 3 years	5	40
* * *		
10 years or more	15	120

Length of continuous service as used on the preceding page shall be based on service at the time the employee's vacation begins. If, later in the calendar year, the employee's anniversary date is reached and such anniversary date entitles the employee to a longer vacation, the employee shall take such additional days of vacation prior to December 31st of that year.

Vacations may be taken at any time during the year except where limited by the preceding paragraph.

Section 5.4. Temporary lost time during an employee's period of employment with the Company of not exceeding twelve (12) consecutive months for layoff or leave of absence shall not be counted against his record of continuous service for the purpose of vacation payment.

Temporary lost time during the employee's period of employment with the Company of not exceeding twenty-four (24) consecutive months for sickness or injury shall not be counted against his record of continuous service for the purpose of vacation or holiday pay.

Article VIII—Leaves of Absence

Section 8.04. Employees absent on pregnancy leaves shall retain seniority up to the leave of absence, but all seniority shall be lost by such employees if they do not return to work three (3) months after the date of delivery. Employees on such leaves of absence are not entitled to any fringe benefits, other than vacation, during such leaves.

POSITION OF THE UNION

Under the provisions of Article V an employee is entitled to vacation pay even though he has been on layoff during the year for which he claims vacation pay. The time periods referred to in Section 5.0 of Article V merely refer to the time he must have worked in the past in order to qualify for vacation pay. Vacation allowances are based in this agreement on a calendar year rather than on a service or anniversary year basis.

Since under the agreement an employee may take his vacation
at any time during the year, an employee who has worked six months
for the company and has received his 1962 vacation may apply in
December of 1962 for his 1963 vacation in January and become entitled to it regardless of whether he has worked in 1963. Had the
parties intended otherwise, they would have established a qualifying
date in the agreement.

Further, under the provisions of Section 5.4 of Article V, an
employee laid off on January 3, 1962 and returning to work on
December 30, 1963 would be entitled to vacation pay for 1963, a
fact readily admitted by the company. These examples indicate the
inequity in the treatment of the grievants, as does the fact that the
company grants vacation pay to employees on pregnancy leaves but
denies it to those on layoff.

In both the 1960 and 1962 contract negotiations the company included employees on layoff in estimating costs for vacations which
were included in the "wage package" settlement. Yet there was no
certainty at either negotiation that these employees on layoff would
ever return to work. In the 1962 negotiations the company unsuccessfully attempted to delete Section 5.4 from the agreement, an
indication that the company recognized it would be liable in just such
a case as this. In those same negotiations the company attempted
unsuccessfully to negotiate for the proration of vacation pay for employees on layoff.

On February 18, 1963 the company sent Mrs. Clare Wirtz her
1963 vacation pay although she had not worked since Easter of 1962.
The union stresses that this is directly on point with the instant
situation.

POSITION OF THE COMPANY

An employee's entitlement to vacation pay rests upon his having
worked during the calendar year in which his vacation pay becomes
due. The words "temporary lost time" in Section 5.4 have no
meaning unless they refer to lost time by employees who are recalled and do return to work. Indeed, the union interpretation of
those words changes the agreement language to read, "the Company
will pay employees laid off vacation pay for one year after layoff."
Obviously, if the parties had intended such a result, they would
have so provided.

If the union prevails, then any employee who is laid off and does not return to work would be entitled to vacation pay for a period of two years after layoff. This is in contradiction to Section 5.4 which was negotiated to assure the laid-off employee that his continuous service would not be broken for the first twelve months of layoff.

During the last contract negotiations the company merely attempted to reduce the "temporary lost time provisions" from a period of twelve months to a period of six months for layoffs and from a period of twenty-four months to a period of twelve months in the case of sickness or injury. These attempts in no way weaken its position in the instant matter. Nor can it be said that a failure to negotiate prorated vacation pay for laid-off employees is inconsistent with its present position on the grievance at hand.

The company cannot recall any deviations from its present application of Article V. But even if the Wirtz situation is as the union presented, then the company in that situation merely did more than it was required to do under the agreement. It should not be penalized now for its generosity.

Suggested Discussion Questions

(a) What is meant by the term "continuous service," and how does the term "temporary lost time" in Article V, Section 5.4 affect it?

(b) If the union's position is upheld, what, if anything, would prevent an employee on layoff for three years who has qualified under the provisions of Article V, Section 5.0 from claiming vacation pay for each of the three years?

(c) Do the "pregnancy" provisions of Article VIII affect the determination of this case?

(d) Should the company's action in paying the eight employees who were laid off on September 6, 1962, recalled on December 15, 1963, and paid their 1963 vacation pay on December 22, 1963 affect the decision in this case?

Bibliography

Dunlop, John T., Collective Bargaining - Principles and Cases (Homewood, Ill.: Richard D. Irwin, Inc., 1949), Part II, "Vacation Provisions," Sect. F, pp. 280-293.

_____ and James J. Healy, Collective Bargaining - Principles and Cases (Homewood, Ill.: Richard D. Irwin, Inc., 1953), Part II, "Vacations and Holidays," Sect. J, pp. 433-456.

Slichter, Sumner H., James J. Healy, and E. Robert Livernash, The Impact of Collective Bargaining on Management (Washington, D. C.: The Brookings Institution, 1960), "Pay for Time Not Worked - Vacations," pp. 426-431; "Paid Holidays," pp. 431-433.

Stone, Morris, Labor Management Contracts at Work (New York: Harper and Row, Publishers, 1961), chap. vii, "Paid Holidays," pp. 112-140; chap. viii, "Vacations and Vacation Pay," pp. 141-156.

Trotta, Maurice S., Labor Arbitration (New York: Simmons-Boardman Publishing Co., 1961), "Issues - Holidays and Holiday Pay," pp. 263-270; "Vacations and Vacation Pay," pp. 360-370.

CHAPTER 6

Work Assignments

Management views the assignment of work as an inherent right emanating out of its position as coordinator of the resources of the firm. Without this right, management fears that its ability to direct the enterprise would be so seriously impaired as to court economic disaster. The employees' quest for job security coupled with their desire for protection from arbitrary decisions in the matter of work assignment has found expression in a number of direct and indirect limitations on management's rights to assign work, among which are the wage, seniority, and work jurisdiction provisions of the collective bargaining agreement.

Management believes that it must retain a certain flexibility in the assignment of work if it is to operate the enterprise effectively and efficiently. Not only are changes in work assignment frequently opposed by the employees, but they often raise rather complex issues of whether such changes violate the implied obligations of management not to thwart or not to deny to employees the benefits which the contract affords.

To what extent, for instance, may management assign tasks formerly carried out by bargaining unit employees to nonbargaining unit employees? While management may regard such assignments as necessary on occasion for efficient operation of the enterprise, the union regards them as direct threats to the job opportunities of bargaining unit employees and a violation of the seniority rights of those employees in that work. The problem is not resolved even in those instances where limitations on nonbargaining unit assumption of bargaining unit duties are specifically provided in the agreement, for usually such prohibitions are hedged by exceptions for emergencies, training, inspection, and the like. The arbitrator is also faced with the question of whether the offense was so small and trifling that any monetary remedy might be considered punitive rather than compensatory.

To what extent may management interchange assignments among bargaining unit employees? Where seniority units are narrow, that is, by occupation or by department, such interchange of assignments may vitally affect the work opportunity of the respective employee groups, and work jurisdiction questions may be bitterly contended. In such situations the respective work claims of each group are frequently difficult to unscramble even in those instances where job descriptions are provided. Do rights in work opportunity flow from the use of certain tools or equipment? Does the location of particular equipment give a particular group of employees the right to its exclusive operation?

May the company temporarily transfer an employee from one job classification to another? If so, what are the rights of the transferred employee in both his temporary assignment and in his regular work? How long may an assignment be considered temporary?

Under what conditions and to what extent may management make permanent changes in the duties of any given job classification? Must such changes be accompanied by physical changes in the manner that work is performed, or can they properly result from mere managerial reorganization of the duties? Did the parties intend to freeze the existing duties of job classifications for the life of the agreement, or did they intend to provide for a rational manner of continually revising the duties of each job classification by accepted industrial engineering standards and job evaluation techniques?

Permanent reassignment of job duties is most bitterly contested when it results in the reduction of crew size, for here the union and the affected employees are confronted with the obvious loss of work opportunity, and it seems to matter little that the surplus crew members are absorbed elsewhere in the operations of the enterprise. Further, a reduction in crew size inevitably means an increase in duties for the remaining members of the crew. Thus, the question arises of what constitutes a fair day's work. Should the standard be that of past practice, or may management unilaterally increase work loads when it feels they have been less than a reasonable work load in the past?

CASES

19. The Atlanta Aviation Company Case

BACKGROUND OF THE CASE

During the latter part of 1962 the company reorganized the duties of the classification, structural test assembler, a labor grade seven classification in the flight test seniority group. Admittedly after reorganization the company had assigned additional duties to this classification, duties not set forth in the job description, and the union had in process numerous grievances claiming that the company was requiring the structural test assembler to perform work out of his classification.

Early in 1963, Mr. James Ivans assumed the post of general foreman of the structural test shop and was confronted with the above problems. After much discussion among company officials, they decided to re-evaluate the classification of structural test assembler. The result of the re-evaluation was to fractionate the classification into two classifications: structural test assembler A and structural test assembler B. The A classification was raised to labor grade nine; the B classification was reduced to labor grade six.

The company in a letter dated July 25, 1963 informed the union of this change and set the effective date of the change as July 29, 1963. It further invited the union to meet for the purpose of establishing the proper seniority groupings for these jobs. On July 29, 1963 the company made the change, promoting all existing structural test assemblers to structural test assemblers A.

The union grieved the action of the company as follows:

The establishment of the job classification of Structural Test Assembler A and B by the company effective 7/29/63 is not a new job within the meaning and understanding of Article V-A, Section 4.

It is the Union's position that this is not a new job, but rather an attempt by the Company to fractionate the jobs already agreed to in the Agreement signed 5/7/63.

Union demands this practice stop immediately and the company pay any and all affected employees such sums of money as is due them according to the Agreement.

It is also the position of the Union, that it is not agreeing to the Labor Grades so assigned. This issue will be taken up at some future date by the Union pending disposition of this grievance.

To which statement the company submitted the following answer:

Structural Test Assembler A—Labor Grade 9, and Structural Test Assembler B—Labor Grade 6, did not exist prior to their establishment on 29 July 1963.

Article V-A, Section 4, clearly provides the manner in which the Union may question the assignment or evaluation of a new job to a labor grade.

The manner in which this grievance has been filed is improper under the existing grievance procedure.

Further discussions were held between the parties, but the grievance was not settled to their mutual satisfaction.

The company pointed out that technically the grievance has not yet progressed through step four of the grievance procedure, and is, therefore, not ripe for arbitration. In view of the fact that the grievance is of long standing, however, the company agreed to arbitrate the matter, with the understanding that the agreement to arbitrate this issue shall not constitute a waiver of its right to insist that future grievances go through the grievance procedure provided in Article V-A of the agreement.

The parties also agreed that the arbitrator shall limit his decision to the narrow issue of whether the company violated the agreement when it unilaterally fractionated the negotiated classification of structural test assembler.

APPLICABLE CONTRACT PROVISIONS

Management Prerogatives

It is recognized that in addition to other functions
and responsibilities which are not otherwise specifically
mentioned in this paragraph, the Company has and will
retain the sole right and responsibility to direct the operations of the Company, and in this connection to determine the number and location of its plants; the product to be
manufactured; the types of work to be performed; the schedules of production; the shift schedules and hours of work;
the methods, processes, and means of manufacturing; to
select, and hire employees; and to make and apply rules
and regulations for production, discipline, efficiency,
and safety. It shall also have the right and responsibility
to demote, discharge, or otherwise discipline any employee for just cause, to lay off because of lack of work
or other cause, and to transfer and promote employees,
unless otherwise hereinafter provided.

Article V-A—Grievance Procedure

Section 4. A claim that under the Hourly Job Rating
Plan a new job has been improperly assigned or evaluated
to a labor grade shall first be taken up by the steward for
the area in which the job is located with the Wage and
Salary Section. Such a claim must be presented to the Wage
and Salary Section by the steward within thirty (30) days of
the assignment or evaluation of the new job to a labor grade.

A copy of the job description and the rate for the job
will be furnished to the steward for the area.

If no satisfactory adjustment of the matter is reached
by the steward and the Wage and Salary Section, it may
then be reduced to writing and processed as a grievance
beginning with Step 2 of the grievance procedure provided
that such grievance is presented at that step not later than
five (5) working days after the decision given by the Wage
and Salary Section. Such written grievance shall state in
detail the specific facts upon which the Union bases its
claim that the job has been improperly evaluated and shall
set forth the specific factors of the evaluation which it
claims are incorrect, giving specific and detailed reasons
for such claim.

POSITION OF THE UNION

The unilateral fractionating of an existing negotiated job classification violates the agreement. There was no bona fide new job
created by the company, and the fact that the company promoted all
existing structural test assemblers into the A classification indicates
that the motive behind the company's action was to make wage savings
in its anticipated increase in the complement of structural test assemblers.

The respective job descriptions show that the respective classifications are substantially identical. Company witness Tyler, who
attempted to distinguish between the classifications, contradicted his
own comparison by admitting that the two classifications performed
essentially the same "nut and bolt" operations. Union witness Jones
testified that there is no difference whatsoever in the duties performed by structural test assemblers A and B on a day-to-day basis.
Work was assigned on the basis of availability of personnel and
priority of the job. The B man who fails to do what Mr. Tyler states
an A man must do is subject to discipline. Under these conditions,
the action of the company was arbitrary and unreasonable.

The action of the company has an impact on the promotional
rights of other employees within the seniority group, since in insti-
tuting the B classification at labor grade six, promotional opportunities and attendant wage increases are worsened, particularly
for the learner group who must progress through the lowest job
classification in the occupation. Structural test assemblers B have
also been disadvantaged in their seniority rights in layoff, since
they may be moved only to lower classifications. While the structural
test assembler A has received an advantage in being advanced to
labor grade nine and slotted into the seniority group at a higher
point, this would have resulted in any event under the re-evaluation,
since admittedly his duties had been increased and a higher labor
grade was in order.

The company should be ordered to reinstate the status quo ante
by reinstating the job classification of structural test assembler, as
revaluated to labor grade nine, and to make whole all employees affected thereby for losses suffered since July 29, 1963.

POSITION OF THE COMPANY

The company may unilaterally create, eliminate, and rearrange job duties between job classifications, when in the company's view such changes are necessary to insure efficient operation. Not only is this an inherent management right, but it has clearly been reserved to the company in the management prerogatives section of the agreement, and is not limited in any manner by other provisions of the agreement.

The definition of a "new job" certainly encompasses the removal of duties from one classification and assigning these duties to another classification. Therefore, it is apparent that the structural test assembler A and the structural test assembler B jobs were new jobs. Thus, the union is confined to the procedure outlined under Article V-A, Section 4 of the agreement concerning disputes over the proper evaluation of these jobs to specific labor grades.

The action was taken by the company in good faith in order to achieve greater efficiency. It permitted the structural test operation to become integrated by requiring the structural test assembler A to perform more complicated assembly and certain jig and fixture work. Greater efficiency was obtained by the use of the B classification when it was not necessary to have work performed of the highest skill of the A classification. Further, the creation of the new jobs did not adversely affect in any manner the structural test assemblers since they were all raised to the A classification which was two labor grades higher than their old labor grade.

The B classification is not required to have the same skill and ability as the A classification. The job description makes clear that the B man is to assist the A man and to perform as directed by the A man. He is neither required nor considered qualified to perform by himself the full range of duties assigned to the A man. Moreover, whether a B man is performing the work of an A man is not involved in the instant case since the only issue is whether the company had the right to create A and B jobs. Further, in this issue, the union is not challenging the validity of the labor grades assigned to either the A or the B classification.

(a) What limitation, if any, on the company's right to fractionate the classification of structural test assembler can be inferred from the fact that specific wages are negotiated for specific classifications in the appendix of the agreement? How might such a limitation be specifically framed by the parties?

(b) Do you think the classifications may be considered as new jobs? Explain.

(c) Suppose the arbitrator found no substantial difference in the duties of the A and B classifications. What effect, if any, would this have on his decision? Explain.

(d) Does the dismissal of this grievance exhaust the union remedies in this problem area? What alternate grievances might the union bring? What is the importance of distinguishing between these issues?

20. The Armbruster Company Case

BACKGROUND OF THE CASE

On May 27, 1965 the company held a regular information meeting with local union officers at which time it discussed certain product problems as well as problems resulting from a sharp increase in forecasted business over the coming months. In order to handle this increase in business the company informed the union that it intended to add some ten or twelve people to the payroll as soon as possible.

At the conclusion of the meeting, Mr. John Baker, chief steward of the union, asked Mr. L. G. Harker, plant manager, whether there was any truth to the rumor that the company intended to establish a third shift. Mr. Harker allegedly replied that "we should keep this as an information meeting." When Mr. Baker persisted that he had been asked about this rumor by other employees, Mr. Harker allegedly stated that all he was interested in was getting enough machinery to have a full complement of personnel on the second shift.

On Tuesday, June 1, 1965 at 9:00 A. M. the union grievance committee was called into the personnel office and handed seven job postings. Six of these postings were for a newly created third shift to be established on Monday, June 7, with the shift hours running from midnight until 7:00 A. M. Local Union President Garfield informed Personnel Manager Moon that the company was obligated to negotiate the wages, hours, and working conditions on the third shift in accordance with the agreement, but Mr. Moon allegedly stated that the company intended to establish the third shift in any event. When questioned about a lunch period, Mr. Moon allegedly stated that third shift employees would receive a paid lunch period and also a 10 per cent shift differential. Mr. Garfield informed the company that the union disagreed with the hours, wages, and conditions established unilaterally by the company and later the same day he filed the following grievance:

> The Union is grieving the unilateral action of the Company in establishing a 3rd shift in violation of present working Agreement.

On June 2, a third step grievance meeting was held at which time the company agreed to postpone establishment of the third shift until June 21. On June 9, it submitted the following answer to the above grievance:

> The establishment of a third shift to meet the production needs of our plant is clearly within the rights of the Management in accordance with our working agreement.
>
> We specifically recognize the Union as the sole and exclusive bargaining agent for the production and maintenance employees whom we would employ on the third shift and we are willing to bargain with you in accordance with Article I, Section 1 of our Contract. The number of production and maintenance employees needed to meet the production needs of this plant is not controlled by the Contract. Meeting our production needs is solely and exclusively the responsibility of the Company as covered under Article II of our Labor Agreement.
>
> We also believe that our proposal is consistent with the provisions contained in Article III, Section 1 of the Agreement.

Therefore your grievance with respect to the establishment of the third shift is denied.

A fourth-step grievance meeting was held on June 15, and further discussions were held on July 8. The company alleges that at the earlier meeting the union conceded the company's right to establish a third shift, but at the latter meeting reversed its position. No resolution of the issue resulted from the meetings, with the consequence that the union filed a demand for arbitration.

APPLICABLE CONTRACT PROVISIONS

Article I—Union Recognition

Section 1. The Company recognizes the Union as the sole and exclusive bargaining agent for all production and maintenance employees with regard to rates of pay, hours of employment, and other conditions of employment.

Article II—Management Rights

Section 1. It is the responsibility of the Management of the Company to maintain discipline and efficiency in the plant. The Management has the sole right to hire and to lay off employees, in accordance with the terms of this Agreement. The right of the Management to discipline and discharge employees for just cause and relieve employees from duty because of inefficiency is expressly recognized subject to the right of appeal through the Grievance Procedure provided in Article XV. In addition, the products to be manufactured, the schedule of production, the methods, processes, and means of manufacturing are solely and exclusively the responsibility of the Company. Previous rights of the Management in the past history of labor relations between the Company and the Union shall be continued.

Article III—Hours and Overtime

Section 1.
(a) The regular work week shall consist of forty (40) hours, five (5) days from Monday to Friday inclusive, consisting of eight (8) hours each day.

(b) Any changes in the regular work day and/or week
as referred to in Section 1 (a) of this Article shall not be
made effective until mutually agreed to by both parties.

Section 2. All work performed in excess of eight (8)
hours in any single day, or in excess of forty (40) hours
in any week and all work performed on Saturdays shall be
paid at the rate of time and one-half.

Article IV—Reporting and Call-In Time

Section 1. Employees who report for work at their
regular starting time on a regular work day shall be given
eight (8) hours work or pay at each employee's regular
rate of pay except as follows:

(a) When notice has been given by the Company either
verbally or by written message at least twelve (12) hours
before the start of the shift or by notice on the bulletin
boards the preceding work day.

(b) When the Company is unable to provide work due
to conditions beyond its control such as lack of power,
fire, earthquakes, floods or similar occurrences.

Article VIII—Wages

Section 7. All employees working on shifts other than
the regular day shift shall receive a rate of pay which will
be ten per cent (10%) above the day hourly rates.

POSITION OF THE UNION

While under the agreement the company has the right to establish
a third shift, the company must negotiate the application of the agreement to the third shift, if that application differs from the manner in
which the agreement is applied to the first and second shifts. Failure
to do so infringes on the union's rights as the collective bargaining
agent for the employees and violates the provisions of Article I,
Section 1 of the agreement.

The application of the agreement terms to third-shift employees
was markedly different from that applied to first- and second-shift
employees. Third-shift employees received a paid lunch period,
whereas employees of the first and second shift did not. Employees
of the third shift received eight hours of pay for six and one-half

hours of work, whereas employees of other shifts received eight hours pay for eight hours of work. Employees of the third shift received premium overtime payments after six and one-half hours of work, whereas first and second shift employees received premium overtime rates only upon completion of their eight-hour shift.

The rights reserved to management under the agreement may not be used in such fashion as to discriminate in favor of certain employees and against other employees. The fundamental purpose of the collective bargaining agreement is to avoid such discrimination, and except for specified exceptions, to insure that all employees are treated alike. The main purpose of the collective bargaining relationship is to discuss problems as they arise. Where, as here, the introduction of a third shift introduces problems arising from variations in hours, in wages, and in premium pay, the company has a responsibility to discuss these with the union and may not make unilateral decisions in these areas.

That the union was handed job postings for a third shift on June 1, 1965, when on May 27, 1965 the company indicated that it had no real intention of establishing a third shift, seems very peculiar. It is even more unusual in the light of the cooperative relationship between the parties which has been characterized in the past by the company's attempting to keep the union informed of production schedules and company needs.

The union requests that the company be ordered to equalize conditions for all employees on all shifts, exclusive of night shift differential, and that the company be ordered to meet and to negotiate on this matter if it desires exceptions for certain employees.

POSITION OF THE COMPANY

Under the agreement the company has the right to establish a third shift. Not only is such right clearly conferred by Article II of the agreement, but also the language of Article VIII, Section 7 providing for a shift premium contemplates that there may be shifts other than the regular day shift. Moreover, the union concedes the company has a general right to establish a third shift.

The company could only schedule third-shift employees for an overall time span of seven hours because other shifts occupied seventeen hours of the day, since both the first and second shifts each spanned eight and one-half hours due to the unpaid lunch perioc

Yet under the agreement, the company must pay employees a minimum of eight hours for working a shift. If the company had sought to get by with paying third-shift employees only seven hours' pay, or six and one-half hours' pay if an unpaid lunch period had been established, it would undoubtedly be in violation of Article III, Section 1(a) and Article IV, Section 1 of the agreement. The union contention that the company action violates the wage scale of the agreement by giving third-shift employees more than the contractually established hourly rate by reason of compensating them at the rate of eight hours' pay for six and one-half hours of work must yield to the overriding idea of the agreement language cited above.

The company strenuously denies that it acted through caprice or in bad faith. The move was dictated by sound business reasons. Owing to the influx of orders and certain quality control problems, as well as the shortage of certain machining equipment, operation of some machines had to be placed on a three-shift operation. There were many discussions of this action, and the company postponed the establishment of the third shift from June 7 to June 22 so that the matter could be completely aired.

Suggested Discussion Questions

(a) The company alleges that during the grievance sessions the union changed its position. To what extent do you think the arbitrator should take into consideration the varying positions of the parties as expressed in grievance sessions? Should the arbitrator allow the admission of evidence concerning the position of one party as expressed in separate meetings, for example, union meetings or supervisor conferences?

(b) Assume for sake of argument that the actions of the company did not violate any express provisions of the agreement. How would you handle the lack of candor on the part of the company at the meeting of May 27, 1965?

(c) To what extent, if at all, is Article IV of the agreement relevant to the issue before the arbitrator?

(d) Suppose the arbitrator finds for the union. Does he have the authority to apply the remedy the union requests? Explain. What alternative remedies are available? Which remedy would you recommend?

21. The Auburn Company Case

BACKGROUND OF THE CASE

The company is engaged in the manufacture of certain wire products. Its Philadelphia plant contains two departments, identified as G department and D department, both of which are concerned with extremely similar winding operations and contain basically similar winding equipment. Employees of the respective departments, however, are separated into departmental job classifications and are carried on different seniority rosters.

On May 21, 1964 a shortage of bobbins developed in the G department. As became apparent, certain existing bobbins of G department wire would have to be rewound on a different type bobbin in order to make bobbins available for the winding of wire then being produced in the G department.

The following day at the beginning of the first shift the foreman of the G department discovered that all machines in the G department capable of performing the rewinding operation were in use. He ascertained, however, that some idle G department rewind equipment could be attached to D department winding machines so that the operation could be carried out on D department machinery.

The foreman instructed Mr. Welsh, an installer, to carry out the installation of G department rewind equipment on department D winding machines. In the course of this work, Mr. Welsh, who was also the chief steward of the union, was informed by the foreman that he would use available G department personnel to carry out the rewinding operation. Mr. Welsh protested that the work in question belonged to the D department and the company should recall qualified employees of the D department then on layoff to perform the rewinding operation.

The foreman of the G department disagreed and subsequently assigned the work to G department employees on the basis that no D department employees were available at the plant to perform the rewinding operation. The assignment in question encompassed one and one-half hours of work on the first shift, seven hours of work on the second shift, and six and one-half hours of work on the third shift.

The union filed the following grievance:

> On May 22, 1964 the Foreman of the Company used
> G Department employees for 1 1/2 hours on the first shift;
> 7 hours on the second shift; and 6 1/2 hours on the third
> shift to perform work in the D Department with employees
> of the G Department, at a time when there were D Depart-
> ment employees on layoff who were capable of performing
> the work involved.

To which grievance the company submitted the following answer:

> On May 22, 1964 it was found that the G Department
> rewinder equipment could not be spared to rewind the
> bobbins and salvage the wire. Since the bobbins were
> needed for immediate use in the G Department, the re-
> wind fixtures were removed from the G Department
> winders and installed on D Department winders. As the
> bobbins were emptied, they were returned to the G Depart-
> ment and wound with G Department wire necessary for the
> G Department braiding operations on overtime for the next
> day.
> This situation constituted an emergency situation and
> encompassed work on only three shifts. However, regard-
> less of the emergency nature of the work, the Company
> insists that the work actually belonged to the employees
> of the G Department.

Unable to resolve the issue to its satisfaction, the union filed a demand for arbitration.

APPLICABLE CONTRACT PROVISIONS

Article III—Work Assignments

Section 1. Except in an emergency, employees are
entitled to perform the work in their regular job classifications and employees on the recall list shall be recalled to work before work in their job classifications is
assigned to any employees in another job classification.

Article IV—Reporting and Call-In Time

Section 2. When an employee reports for work at the
customary time without being notified to the contrary by
the Company or is entitled to report for work at such time
and is assigned to no work or works for a lesser period
than four hours, payment shall be made for a minimum of
four hours time at the hourly rate customarily paid the
employee.

POSITION OF THE UNION

The rewinding operation was performed upon winding machines
located in the D department. These machines had merely been adjusted to perform the work in question, and therefore the work was
properly that of D department employees.

No emergency existed in the instant situation since the foreman
of the G department knew on May 21, 1964 that the rewinding operation would have to be performed. The company had sufficient time
to survey its equipment and personnel and determine whether the
operation could be performed in the G department. If it misjudged
the availability of that equipment and/or those personnel, then the
employees of the D department, including those on layoff, should
not be penalized by the company's error in judgment.

Article III clearly provides that D department employees are
entitled to perform D department work. In consequence, the company
was obligated to call in employees of the D department who were on
layoff to perform the work to which employees of that department
were entitled.

POSITION OF THE COMPANY

Although the foreman of the G department was aware that the
wire in question would have to be rewound, he did not become aware
of the unavailability of G department machinery to perform the rewinding operation until the morning of May 22. These bobbins were
needed to keep G department personnel employed. Since it had
available employees in that department to carry out the rewinding
operation, it resorted to their use in an emergency situation.

Even in the absence of an emergency situation, the company

was within its rights in assigning a G department employee to perform the rewinding operation. The wire to be rewound was G department wire. The rewind equipment which was used was also that of
the G department. The bobbins involved were those of the G department. The mere fact that this work was carried out on D department
winding machines, owing entirely to the unavailability of G department
machines, is not sufficient to convert such work into that entitled to
be carried out by employees of D department.

Suggested Discussion Questions

(a) Can the company action be properly defended as one arising out
     of an emergency situation? Explain showing clearly what you
     believe are essential ingredients of an emergency.

(b) Suppose employees of both department G and department D had
     been available. Would this change your determination of whether
     a contract violation had been committed? Explain.

(c) What criteria would you use to determine whether the rewind
     operation was properly the work of department G or department
     D employees?

(d) Suppose neither equipment nor personnel were available in
     department G and the work was carried out by department D
     personnel. Would department G employees have a valid
     grievance?

22. The Rumford Company Case

BACKGROUND OF THE CASE

On October 1, 1963 the company started to install an under-
ground conduit system of Transite pipe, a concrete composition
pipe constructed in sections which contain slip joints for easy
combination of segments. The system was to be 920 feet in length
and was to serve as a water repellent housing for electrical cable.
Initially the company assigned employees in the classification

of laborer to dig a three-foot ditch, lay the pipe, perform the joining, and fill in the ditch. Since there were insufficient laborers to complete the construction in the time required to meet the scheduled completion date, the company subsequently assigned off-shift employees on an overtime basis in the classifications of oiler, mill helper, tank man, truck driver, coal mill man, fillerman, and pipeman to assist the laborers.

When these operations had been completed on October 20, 1965, the company assigned electricians to pull the electrical cable through the Transite pipe conduit and to carry out the other work necessary to complete the electrical installation. Since electricians were already busy on other work, the assignment was on an overtime basis at premium rates of pay. The electricians were allegedly unaware that the preparatory work had been assigned to other occupational classifications, and upon receiving the assignment filed the following grievance:

> We feel that electrical work was done by Laborers and other occupations in the form of laying Transite pipe on overtime, which work belongs exclusively to the Electrician's job classification.

Unable to resolve the issue to its satisfaction, the union filed a demand for arbitration.

APPLICABLE CONTRACT PROVISIONS

Article XX—Management

Section 1. The Management of the plant and affairs of the Company, including but not limited to the establishment of reasonable rules and regulations, the direction of the working forces, the right to hire, . . . the introduction of new or improved production methods or facilities is vested exclusively in the Company, subject only to such limitations as may be specifically imposed by this Agreement.

Article XXIV—Wages

Section 10. If work of a higher paid classification is required of an employee, he shall receive the higher rate

of pay for such time as he works on the higher paid job,
but if he is temporarily assigned to a job taking a lower
rate of pay, his rate of pay shall not be reduced.

POSITION OF THE UNION

While laborers have in the past dug and filled ditches during the
course of laying Transite pipe, the actual laying of the pipe and the
joining of the lengths together is work normally performed by
electricians. Unless the laid pipe is properly slip jointed, water
can get to the cable and damage the electrical system, and consequently it is inherently the work of electricians.

Article XX of the agreement does not give the company the
right to assign any employee to perform any job regardless of
capability or skill. By assigning the laying and joining lengths of
Transite pipe to laborers and other classifications, the company
is undermining the work of electricians. The underlying motive on
the part of the company is to reduce the labor costs involved in the
installation.

POSITION OF THE COMPANY

The digging of ditches and the laying of Transite pipe therein is
clearly unskilled work. Transite pipe is merely slip jointed, that
is, it is so constructed that the end of one section of pipe may be
forced over the end of another section. The inherent skills of an
electrician are not involved. Electricians, on the other hand, have
been consistently assigned to carry out the electrical aspects of the
operation, namely the pulling of the cable through the conduit and
the installing and connecting of the cable to various electrical
equipment. Electricians, in the instant situation, were given this
assignment at overtime rates of pay.

Past practice also supports the company's contention that the
laying and slip-joining of Transite pipe is work normally performed
by employees in the laborer classification. The following incidents
were cited by the company without objection by the union.

1. During 1957 Transite pipe was laid from the Cell
House to the Thickener, a distance of 125 feet. The work

was performed by Laborers and Electricians. Electrical
cable was pulled at the same time.

2. During 1959 Transite pipe was laid from the Silo
to the Coal Mill. The installation was performed by
Laborers and Electricians. Electrical cable was pulled
at the same time.

3. On or about July, 1960 Transite pipe was laid
from the Coal Mill to the Rejects Plant by Laborers and
Electricians. Electrical cable was pulled at the same
time.

4. On or about March, 1961 Transite pipe was laid
from the front of the Kiln Room to the Multiclones. The
pipe was installed by Laborers. Electricians installed the
cable at a later time.

5. On or about March, 1962 Transite pipe was installed from the Crane Storage area to the Sub-Station by
Laborers and Electricians. In this instance the Transite
pipe was slipped over the electrical cable before the cable
was finally hooked up.

These instances indicate that the work in question is not exclusively
that of electricians but has been performed in whole or in part by
laborers. Moreover, the only times that the laborers and electricians
worked in consort were in those instances where the cable was being
pulled through the pipe at the same time that the pipe was being laid.
The company also points to the fact that no electrician was present
at the hearing to present firsthand testimony.

Article XX of the agreement provides that the company has the
sole right to direct the working forces. There are no provisions
in the agreement which limit in any way the company's right to do
what it did.

Suggested Discussion Questions

(a) Does the management clause give the company an unrestricted
right to assign employees? What express or implied limitations
might be forwarded by the union as restrictions on such a right?

(b) To what extent should the arbitrator be influenced by the failure
     of electricians to appear as witnesses during the hearing?
     Explain.

(c) During the course of the hearing the parties vacillated between
     whether the work was "exclusively" performed by electricians or
     "normally" performed by electricians. Is there a difference be-
     tween these criteria? Explain. Which criterion should be ac-
     cepted by the arbitrator in this situation? Explain.

(d) To what extent do the instances mentioned by the company con-
     stitute a past practice? Explain.

23. The Lewiston Company Case

BACKGROUND OF THE CASE

The union and the company experienced a long strike during the
summer and early fall of 1962. In settlement of that strike a memorandum of agreement was executed on October 3, 1962. The memorandum of agreement amended certain specific contract terms and,
in addition, included a memorandum of understanding regarding the
utilization of manpower. The memorandum of understanding reads,
in part, as follows:

5. Utilization of manpower

The Company has stated that it must have flexibility in
order to make full utilization of manpower. This is necessary in order that the Company may stay in business and
be competitive.

The Union representatives agree that the UNION and the
employees will cooperate with the Company in order to
bring this about.

The Union and employer representatives have engaged in
long discussions of their intent and the following are some
examples of the Company and Union expression of intent
to bring this about.

1. The Union intends to cooperate with the Company in

reassigning employees to get over jam-ups, emergency situations, and so forth.

2. The Union recognizes that the Company shall make every effort to stop waste of manpower, and that to this end it may have to combine jobs and take other reasonable and necessary measures.

3. It is not the intent of the Company to use temporary transfers as a device to prevent people being recalled from layoff.

4. It is not the intent of the Company to put an employee on a job that he cannot do with intent to discharge him on the basis of lack of ability.

5. It is the intent of the Company that employees temporarily transferred will continue to accrue seniority in their own department.

6. It is not the intent of the Company to transfer employees from their own jobs and have other employees do their work.

7. The Company agrees that an employee who is temporarily doing work out of his classification shall be paid either the rate for the job on which he is working or his own rate, whichever is higher.

In substance, this understanding was sought by the company in order to regain certain rights in the utilization of its manpower. These rights, for the most part, had become eroded away by contrary practices which had grown up over an extended period of time, an interim which spanned the life of a number of collective bargaining agreements.

Prior to the time of the strike the traffic department at the Basin Street Plant consisted of two bargaining unit employees and two supervisors. After the strike as a result of a reduction in the volume of work only one bargaining unit employee, Mr. William Ewell, was recalled to work. Mr. Ewell returned to work on October 5, 1962. On October 9th and almost daily thereafter through the middle of January, 1963, Mr. Ewell was assigned during the afternoons, from approximately 1:00 P.M. until 3:30 P.M. or 4:00 P.M. to check and tag drums on the chemical platform, work

which is admittedly part of a different seniority area, the shipping
department. During this time at least one employee of the shipping
department was on layoff status.

While this assignment was allegedly made because Mr. Ewell
had idle time in his regular job of traffic clerk, on occasion a supervisor had to assume a small portion of Mr. Ewell's work as traffic
clerk during his assignment to the chemical platform. The work
assumed was that of preparing a report of outbound railroad cars
and the calling in of such a report to the railroad.

The union grieved that this assignment violated both the agreement and the memorandum of understanding regarding the utilization
of manpower in a number of respects. Unable to resolve the grievance to its satisfaction, the union filed a demand for arbitration.

APPLICABLE CONTRACT PROVISIONS

Article I—Recognition

3. It is mutually understood and agreed that any Superin-
    tendents, Department Heads, Foremen, and Supervisors
    above excluded from the bargaining unit, are not to en-
    gage in or participate in any operation performed by
    workers who are members of the UNION.

Article V—Work Assignments

3. (n) Foremen, forewomen, and other supervisory em-
    ployees above excluded from the bargaining unit shall
    not be permitted to perform the work of any other em-
    ployee when their doing of such work will cause loss
    of working time to any other employee. All leaders
    shall be working leaders, unless exempted.

POSITION OF THE UNION

The assumption of Mr. Ewell's work by supervisory personnel
in the traffic department violated both Article I and Article V,
Section 3(n) of the agreement. Although prior to the strike, supervisors performed some bargaining unit work in the traffic department, this occurred only in those situations where bargaining unit
employees were busy with their regular duties.

The assignment of Mr. Ewell to the chemical platform also violated Section 3 of the memorandum of understanding regarding utilization of manpower by using the temporary transfer of Mr. Ewell to avoid the recall of shipping department employees. At the time of Mr. Ewell's transfer to the chemical platform, at least one shipping department employee was on layoff status. Moreover, since supervision in the traffic department performed parts of Mr. Ewell's work during his transfer, Section 6 of the memorandum was also clearly violated.

The union, therefore, requests that compensation be paid to the shipping department employee who should have been recalled to perform the work performed by Mr. Ewell on the chemical platform.

POSITION OF THE COMPANY

No provision in the agreement purports to restrict the company's right to assign Mr. Ewell to the performance of shipping department work on the chemical platform. If by past practice such a restriction existed which would have precluded the assignment in question, such restriction has been clearly modified by the memorandum of understanding regarding the utilization of manpower. The parties have specifically agreed that the company can make every effort to stop waste of manpower, that it can combine jobs, and take other reasonable and necessary measures. The company acted reasonably and in good faith in utilizing Mr. Ewell to get the shipping work completed. It involved two and one-half to three hours of work per day. Obviously to bring back an employee for a full day would create a waste of manpower, precisely what the union had agreed was not necessary. The company analyzed the work in the traffic department and found that Mr. Ewell had idle time. It was conscientiously endeavoring to use this idle time.

The company is aware of the contractual restriction prohibiting supervisors from performing bargaining unit work. The provision, however, has as its purpose the protection of bargaining unit work, and it cannot be said that the company's action in this instance impaired the preservation of that principle. When the company assigned Mr. Ewell to the chemical platform, it did not plan to have a supervisor perform any part of his work. A large part of the outbound report is made up in the morning and called in to the railroad at the end of the day. Frequently during the afternoon minor additions, deletions, and adjustments are reported to the traffic office to reflect the latest shipment conditions, and these had to be taken down by supervision in Mr. Ewell's absence. In those instances where the changes were large, Mr. Ewell did not have sufficient time to complete the report, and supervision started it in his absence, as it also did when his work on the chemical platform engaged him beyond his contemplated 3:30 P.M. return. In most instances Mr. Ewell returned to the traffic department at 3:30 P.M. and had ample time to complete his report. Thus, the amount of work performed by supervision was minimal, and had little, if any, effect on the bargaining unit. The company emphasized that traffic work in all other plants is carried out solely by nonbargaining unit personnel.

Suggested Discussion Questions

(a) Do you think the temporary transfer of Mr. Ewell violated Section 3 of the memorandum of understanding regarding the utilization of manpower? Carefully develop a set of reasons for your position.

(b) The company claims that any violation of the prohibition on supervisory assumption of bargaining unit work was, if at all, de minimis. What is meant by de minimis? Do you think that this doctrine can be employed in this specific situation? Explain.

(c) The company also argues that any assumption of Mr. Ewell's work by supervision in no way impaired the principle underlying the purpose of the restrictions upon supervisory performance of bargaining unit work, that is, the protection of that work for the bargaining unit employee. Do you agree? Explain carefully.

(d) To what extent, if any, does the memorandum of understanding concerning the utilization of manpower modify or amend the express provisions of the agreement? Explain.

Bibliography

Bailer, L. H., "Right to Assign Employees in One Job Classification to Jobs in Another Classification," Industrial and Labor Relations Review, Vol. XVI, No. 2 (January, 1963), pp. 200-204.

Davis, Pearce, "Arbitration of Work Rules Disputes," The Arbitration Journal, Vol. XVI, No. 2 (1961), pp. 51-60.

Fairweather, O., "Implied Restrictions on Work Movement—the Pernicious Crow of Labor Contract Construction," Notre Dame Lawyer, Vol. XXXVIII, No. 5 (August, 1963), pp. 518-554.

Rubin, M. L., "The Right to Split Jobs and Assign Work to Another Classification," Industrial and Labor Relations Review, Vol. XVI, No. 2 (January, 1963), pp. 205-207.

Stone, Morris, Labor Management Contracts At Work (New York: Harper & Row, Publishers, 1961), chap. v, "Foremen and Supervisors," pp. 73-95.

_____, Management Freedom and Job Security (New York: Harper & Row, Publishers, 1964), chap. iv, "Erosion of the Bargaining Unit," pp. 67-99; chap. v, "Jurisdiction Over Work," pp. 100-126; chap. vi, "The Integrity of Jobs and Classifications," pp. 127-167; chap. vii, "Work Load Disputes," pp. 168-203.

Wallen, Saul R., "The Arbitration of Work Assignment Disputes," Industrial and Labor Relations Review, Vol. XVI, No. 2 (January, 1963), pp. 193-199.

_____, "The Silent Contract vs. Expressed Provisions: The Arbitration of Local Working Conditions," Collective Bargaining and the Arbitrator's Role, Proceedings of the Fifteenth Annual Meeting, National Academy of Arbitrators, Pittsburgh, Pa., January 24-26, 1962 (Washington, D. C.: Bureau of National Affairs, 1962), pp. 117-147.

CHAPTER 7

Seniority

The principle of seniority is that of giving preference in employment opportunities to those employees with greater length of service. In at least one respect collective bargaining provisions conferring seniority rights upon employees differ from other benefits conferred by the collective bargaining agreement. Under the seniority provisions preference can only be conferred upon one employee by an equivalent denial of benefits to another. Unlike union demands for higher wages or improved working conditions, issues which benefit all bargaining unit employees, seniority provisions merely determine *who* among the bargaining unit employees gets the available opportunities. Seniority provisions do not create jobs, but merely allocate them.

One aspect of this problem is that frequently no common agreement exists within a union as to what type of seniority plan should be negotiated, or even after the negotiation of specific seniority language in a collective bargaining agreement, how such language shall be interpreted and applied. Considerable friction can result within the union itself on these issues. Seniority issues are often passed on to arbitration because they are "too hot to handle" in earlier steps of the grievance procedure. In addition, the union is on occasion found in the anomalous position of advancing one employee's claim in one grievance, only to advance later the counterclaim of another employee who has been injured by the successful prosecution of the original claim.

Another reason for the many problems in applying the seniority provisions of the collective bargaining agreement to concrete situations is that while the idea of senority—giving preference in employment opportunities to those employees with greater length of service—is easily understood, attempts to apply it to the situations which arise frequently become quite complex. If we take the above definition of seniority—giving preference in employment opportunities to those employees with greater length of service—some of the complexities can be revealed by asking the questions: What employment opportunities? What service? How much preference?

While one may say, broadly speaking, that seniority rights are most commonly applied to job opportunities during a reduction in force and to promotional opportunities, even at this point a series of problems develop. Specifically, what is a layoff? Does a layoff result when no one is actually removed from the payroll, but all employees are absorbed on lower-paying jobs? Similarly what constitutes a promotional opportunity? Does a promotional opportunity result when an employee calls in sick, or when a new job requires only three days of work?

Employment opportunities are also frequently limited to those within a given job classification or to those within a given department. On the other hand, they may be broadened to include all opportunities within a given plant or throughout the company. This is often referred to as the seniority unit. In interpretation of these questions, the arbitrator must determine from the language of the agreement over what span of jobs a given employee may exercise his seniority.

Although seniority was defined as giving preference in job opportunity to those employees with greater length of service, what specific service is intended is not always clear. The service taken into consideration may be time spent on a given job, in a given department, in a given plant, or with a particular company. Therefore, the arbitrator must glean from the agreement language the intentions of the parties in this respect.

All sorts of problems result from questions of how much preference may be accorded seniority relative to an employee's ability, both physical and mental, to carry out the job requirements. Even under the so-called "straight-seniority" provisions, wherein ability is accorded no consideration in the contract language, arbitrators have usually required a minimum of ability to carry out the requirements of the job. To what extent, however, should ability considerations be introduced to override considerations of seniority? Should ability or seniority be the determining factor?

Moreover, to what ability does the contract refer? Is it the present ability or the potential ability of the employee which is relevant? Ability to perform what range of duties of the job in question? If the job is expected to change in the future, may the company require an ability over and above that currently needed to carry out the present tasks of the job? What are proper criteria of ability? Even practical demonstrations such as trial periods may result in questionable measurements of ability.

Frequently, the seniority provisions of the agreement are also utilized as guarantees against allegedly arbitrary action on the part of companies where disputes over the physical fitness of employees are concerned. The question frequently arises as to what extent the seniority provisions prevent the company from refusing to reassign or to recall employees who are alleged to possess physical ailments which prevent their satisfactory accomplishment of the job without fear of injury to themselves or others.

CASES

24. The Applied Products Company Case

BACKGROUND OF THE CASE

In March of 1963, the company contemplated a reduction in force in its maintenance department although job opportunities in other departments of the plant would provide sufficient work for those who were demoted out of the department. Thereafter, the company presented a plan for demotion along the lines of least departmental seniority, which plan was favored by a majority of union representatives. Agreement on this plan, however, was not unanimous, nor was there a mutual agreement in writing that the plan was acceptable.

On March 11, 1963, the company made the reduction in force, affecting the following employees:

Jr. Mechanics	Date of Hire	Date of Dept. Assignment
Eugene Abel	8-10-59	8-10-59
Salvatore Baker	9-14-59	9-14-59
Delmar Charles	11-30-59	11-30-59
William Davis	10-20-59	7-30-60
Kenneth Edwards	9- 8-59	3-19-62
Victor Fox	9- 8-59	3-19-62
Leon George	9- 8-59	3-19-62
Marlin Hughes	10-26-59	3-19-62
Harold Ireland	10-26-59	3-19-62
General Mechanic		
Paul Jenkins	9- 9-62	5-18-62

In the departmental reduction in force, employees Abel, Baker, Charles, and Davis were retained as junior mechanics, and em-

ployees Edwards, Fox, George, Hughes, and Ireland were demoted
into the lower-rated job, mechanic "B." Mr. Jenkins was also demoted into the job of mechanic "B," but the union entertained a
grievance on his behalf which grievance was settled in the course of
the grievance procedure by the reassignment of Jenkins to the job of
junior mechanic and the concurrent demotion of Abel to the job of
mechanic "B."

Following this readjustment of the labor force employees,
Edwards, Fox, and George filed similar grievances claiming that
the company had not properly applied the plant-wide seniority provisions of the labor agreement, and that their respective seniority
rights to the job of junior mechanic had been violated. The company
denied these claims and the matter went to arbitration.

APPLICABLE CONTRACT PROVISIONS

Section 7

A. Seniority Status of Employees:
   1. The parties recognize that promotional opportunity
       and job security in the event of promotions, de-
       crease of forces, demotions resulting from de-
       crease of forces, and calls to return to work after
       layoffs should increase in proportion to length of
       continuous service and that in the administration
       of this Section the intent will be that wherever
       practicable, full consideration shall be given to
       continuous service in such cases.
   2. In recognition, however, of the responsibility of
       Management for the efficient operation of the works,
       it is understood and agreed that in all cases of pro-
       motion . . . decrease of forces, demotions re-
       sulting from decrease of forces, the following
       factors as listed below shall be considered; how-
       ever, only where the first two (2) factors are
       relatively equal shall continuous service be the
       determining factor.
       (a) ability to perform the work
       (b) physical fitness
       (c) continuous service

C. Plant-wide Seniority
  1. The unit for the application of the seniority factors
     shall be plant-wide with respect to promotions, de-
     crease of forces which result in layoff for more
     than five (5) normal work days, demotions re-
     sulting from such decrease in forces, and recalls
     to work after such layoffs. . . .

D. Departmental Seniority
  1. In cases of layoffs of from one (1) to not more than
     five (5) normal workdays, the unit for application
     of the seniority factors shall be each Department
     by shift. The seniority provisions of this Agree-
     ment shall not apply to layoffs of less than one (1)
     normal work day.

POSITION OF THE COMPANY

The company contends that the instant situation is not covered
by the agreement and, therefore, the company cannot be found in
violation of the agreement. It points out that Section 7-C does not
apply since, first, the demotions of the grievants were for more
than five normal work days and, second, no layoffs were involved.
The provisions of Section 7-B do not cover the instant situation,
since there were no layoffs, and such section specifies the procedure resulting from layoffs. The company cannot be accused
of violating the agreement when the agreement does not require
consideration of either departmental or plant-wide seniority factors.

In demoting the grievants, the company acted reasonably and in
good faith. Several days before the demotion, company representatives met union representatives to discuss the most acceptable
method of selecting which employees would be demoted and which
ones would be retained as junior mechanics. The approach recom-
mended by the union and favored by all but one of the four union
representatives present was subsequently adopted by the company.

In practice, certain junior mechanics have been assigned to
perform certain more or less specialized types of work falling
within the broad range of this wage rate classification, while other
junior mechanics were used more as general utility men working on
whatever assignments came up. Baker, Charles, and Jenkins were

specialists in lubrication, automotive maintenance, and welding respectively. Davis was a specialist, on a seasonal basis, in air-conditioning. The others, Abel, Edwards, Fox, George, Hughes, and Ireland were used on general assignments.

The company's retention of the four incumbents was based on their superior skills within the scope of the junior mechanic classification and was consistent with the seniority factors outlined in the agreement.

(1) Employee Baker had been carrying out the oiling and greasing in the plant and boiler room for a period of about three and one-half years, more or less exclusively. His performance was regarded as very competent by supervision. He had been instructed by engineers from major oil companies as to which types of oils to use for particular equipment, the reasons therefor, and where, when, and how to apply the lubricants. Although the machinery has been tagged to make proper lubrication procedures easier, at the time of the company's action the machinery was not tagged. None of the grievants had any experience in this capacity with the company except employee Edwards, who had two months' experience in the fall of 1959 when very little equipment was operating and when much of the present equipment had not yet been installed.

(2) Employee Charles was retained for his superior ability to perform the automotive maintenance. He had eight years' previous experience indicated on his employment application and had been predominantly occupied in performing this work for the company since March, 1960. His performance was deemed to be excellent by supervision. None of the other grievants had ever demonstrated any automotive maintenance ability in his work for the company.

(3) Employee Jenkins' general mechanical ability was substantially superior to that of the grievants as evidenced by the fact that he was hired as a general mechanic, a higher classification than a junior mechanic, and the skill and ability he possessed as a general mechanic made him a superior junior mechanic. This was precisely the position advanced by the union in processing his grievance when he sought to bump into the junior mechanic classification. His outstanding general mechanical ability has been recognized and agreed to in the settlement of his prior grievance.

(4) Employee Davis was retained because he alone of all the junior mechanics had training and experience in operating the air-

conditioning equipment. Although in March of 1963 the need for
Davis' superior ability in this regard was not immediate, it was
presumably foreseeable as the summer months approached. During
1962 he was employed on this work for three and a half months.
Not having him available as a junior mechanic when the air-conditioning need would arise, would cause the company considerable in-
convenience.

POSITION OF THE UNION

The retention of employees with less plant-wide seniority in the
junior mechanic classification is a violation of the seniority provisions of the agreement. Under Paragraph 1 of Section 7-A of the
agreement, the company and the union agreed that full consideration
would be given to continuous service in the matter of increasing or
decreasing forces. The company, therefore, did not have the right
to reduce senior employees and retain the less senior since the
company has not demonstrated that the efficiency of the plant would,
in any way, be lessened by such a move.

The union points to the fact that the jobs in question are not
particularly skilled jobs, but entail, essentially, assistance to other
skilled employees in higher classifications. All of the grievants
have the ability to do the work required by this classification. There
is nothing unusual about the lubrication job, and the machinery is
currently tagged to indicate the parts to be lubricated, the type of
lubricant necessary, and the time period between lubrications. The
company was unable to demonstrate that any of the grievants could
not have performed this work satisfactorily. With respect to the
automotive maintenance job, this too entailed only the simplest type
of maintenance. All of the grievants testified that they frequently
performed such work on their own cars at home. Although the union
admits it processed a grievance for employee Jenkins in his efforts
to bump into the job of junior mechanic, it insists that it did this
unwillingly and only because of its responsibilities to represent the
claim of any member, regardless of its position on the grievance
in question. The retention of employee Davis for his presumed
ability to handle air-conditioning is a smoke screen for its illegal
action, since Davis was not, at the time of the grievance, and has
not, up to the time of the arbitration proceeding, been performing
any air-conditioning work.

The union requests that the grievants, employees Edwards, George, and Fox be placed on the job of junior mechanic, and that they be paid the difference between the earnings of that job and the actual earnings which they have received since March 11, 1963.

Suggested Discussion Questions

(a) What differences would it make in the arbitrator's resolution of the above issue had the collective bargaining agreement contained only Section 7-A, and been mute on the specific procedure to be followed? What additional information might be sought by the arbitrator?

(b) How would the elimination of Paragraph 2 of Section 7-A from the collective bargaining agreement affect the outcome in the case? What changes in the company's evaluation of ability might be required?

(c) Does the fact that the union unwillingly processed a previous grievance on behalf of employee Jenkins affect its right to process a grievance in the situation described above where the effect of such processing would lead to a counter-result?

(d) What factors might influence the arbitrator's remedy, if any, in the case?

25. The Babylonian Company Case

BACKGROUND OF THE CASE

Mr. Charles E. Kay, an employee of the Babylonian Company since 1958, was laid off on December 16, 1962. On November 27, 1963, he received a notice to report for work on December 2, 1963 since there now existed work to which his seniority entitled him. Upon reporting to the company on December 2, 1963, he was examined by the company doctor, a practice in accord with company-wide policy, and was found to be suffering from high blood pressure and obesity. He was rejected for work and told to take off con-

siderable weight, after which he would probably be accepted for the
job. On December 9, 1963, Mr. Kay was again examined and rejected. On December 23, 1963, Mr. Kay was examined a third
time, and the company doctor, after noting a considerable weight
loss and a reduction of blood pressure, accepted him for employment.

The evidence indicated that Mr. Kay had a history of obesity
and high blood pressure. He was turned down for these reasons
when he had originally applied for work for the company in 1958,
but after bringing down his weight (and blood pressure) he was
accepted for employment. The medical history of his examinations
during December was as follows:

Height	Blood Pressure	Weight
Dec. 2, 1963—5' 8 1/2"	165/105	234
Dec. 9, 1963— "	155/108	220
Dec. 23, 1963— "	132/ 80	209

The company physician, Dr. Robert Love, testified that
company policy imposed strict weight and blood pressure limitations
on prospective employees. Under these limitations, Mr. Kay ideally
should not weigh more than 160-165 pounds, although Dr. Love admitted that variations of 15 to 20 per cent were not abnormal, if not
accompanied by high blood pressure. Dr. Love admitted that he was
unaware of Mr. Kay's job duties and felt that in this situation they
were irrelevant. While he could not prognosticate that any of the
following disablements was highly probable, Dr. Love feared that
with increasing weight gain, Mr. Kay's blood pressure would rise:
"With blood pressure rise, fainting spells, dizziness, and possible
stroke, heart attack, or heart failure are all feared." Dr. Love
further admitted that he was particularly hard on Mr. Kay in an
effort to get Mr. Kay to recognize the seriousness of his condition
and to take care of it. "All he had to do was eat less." In fact,
Dr. Love was quick to point out that he approved Mr. Kay for employment, although he was above company limits, because the employee was "showing his good intentions."

Subsequent to his return to work, Mr. Kay filed a grievance requesting that he be paid all monies lost for the period from December
2, 1963 through December 23, 1963. The parties were unable to resolve this grievance satisfactorily in the grievance procedure, with

the consequence that the parties agreed on the following submission
of the dispute to arbitration:

> Did the Company violate Article VII, Section 9 of the
> Agreement when it refused C. E. Kay return to work
> on December 2, 1963 ? If so, what is the Company's
> financial liability ?

APPLICABLE CONTRACT PROVISIONS

Article VII

Section 9. In the event of layoff, employees with the
least seniority shall be laid off, in accordance with the
procedure outlined below, if employees with greater
seniority can perform the available work without being
trained. In recall to work after layoff, employees on
layoff with the greatest seniority on a plant-wide Bargaining Unit basis shall be recalled first, subject to their
ability to perform the available work without being trained.

POSITION OF THE COMPANY

The grievant's condition was a definite detriment to his health.
While undoubtedly there are employees at work who are overweight,
Mr. Kay's case was not one of being overweight alone, but of being
excessively overweight, which caused high blood pressure, and
more specifically, an alarming blood pressure rise at the time he
was examined on December 2, 1963 and December 9, 1963. Mr.
Kay also had a history of hypertension. When he applied for work
in September, 1958, he was rejected because of hypertension.
Not until the grievant had brought his weight down to within
reason did his blood pressure return to normal. The concern of
Dr. Love over this condition was evidenced by the fact that he requested the grievant to weigh in and have his blood pressure recorded weekly from December 23, 1963 until July, 1964, a period
of over six months. The company submits that the three-week
period in question, from December 2, 1963 to December 23, 1963,
served to ameliorate Mr. Kay's physical condition which was a
clear and present danger to his health, and as such the action of
the company was clearly justified.

POSITION OF THE UNION

The refusal of the company to return Mr. Kay to work violates his seniority rights which are protected under Article VII, Section 9 of the collective bargaining agreement. Unless an employee suffers a disability which obviously prevents him from performing his work, he must be returned to work in accordance with the above contract provision. The company did not even challenge the fact that Mr. Kay could perform his job. Seniority rights cannot be set aside because the company thinks it is desirable for everyone to have normal weight and blood pressure. Nor has the company the right to superimpose a company medical policy over the negotiated terms of the collective bargaining agreement.

Suggested Discussion Questions

(a) To what extent, if any, should an arbitrator be guided by expert medical testimony?

(b) What differences can be noted in the determination of whether an employee has physical ability to carry out a given job as contrasted with a determination of whether he has technological and mental ability to perform that job? What similarities are there?

(c) Suppose Mr. Kay had not been able to reduce his weight and/or blood pressure and had not been re-employed by the company. Would this affect your answer to a grievance asserting essentially the same facts?

(d) To what extent would a showing by the company that its treatment of Mr. Kay was in strict accordance with its company-wide medical policy at all plants of the company influence your final decision?

26. The Cyclonic Corporation Case

BACKGROUND OF THE CASE

Owing to a reduction in force, employee Edward J. Martin, a storekeeper A in the die storage department, exercised his bumping rights on the basis of his plant-wide seniority and attempted to claim the job storekeeper A in the main press department displacing employee Charles Newman.

At the end of the first day, the foreman of the main press department, Mr. George Oglethorpe, informed Mr. Martin that he was not displaying sufficient ability to retain the job and that he would be laid off. Mr. Martin requested that he be given more time to prove his ability and on specific instructions from higher management authority, Foreman Oglethorpe was ordered "to get Martin back for a fair trial." Employee Martin was retained for the full seven-day trial period, the maximum allowed under the agreement. During this period, the displaced former incumbent of the job in question was also retained on the department payroll. At the end of the seven-day period Martin was laid off for lack of ability, the layoff slip stating: "Probably a storekeeper, but not in this department."

Mr. Martin protested that he was not given a fair trial in accordance with the spirit and intent of the collective bargaining agreement. The company denied that the trial period was unfair and the matter went to arbitration.

APPLICABLE CONTRACT PROVISIONS

Article V

Section 13. If at any time during the application of the above seniority rules the Company should question the qualifications or ability of an employee, he shall have the right to request a fair but minimum trial period to prove his ability before forfeiting his right to the job in question. Said trial period to be a maximum of seven (7) working days.

POSITION OF THE COMPANY

The company contends that the mere fact that employee Martin had experience as a storekeeper in one department of the company is no assurance that he is qualified in another department. The company points out that the dies in the main press department are much larger and the recordkeeping is considerably different. A trial period is not established for the purpose of learning the job or developing ability, but rather for the demonstration of existing ability.

Mr. Martin, on the very first day, showed an inability to find needed dies in the storeroom, the basic element of the job of storekeeper. On another occasion, the foreman discovered a number of die setters sitting around while Mr. Martin looked in vain for a set of dies which were already set up on the presses. This fact could have been easily ascertained, the company argues, from consulting a list of dies already set. The company further maintains that the work of storekeeper in the main press department is extremely simple. A "night list" is prepared for the storekeeper, which list shows whether dies are on the presses or in storage. Dies are also painted with identification numbers so that they should be readily spotted from a distance of twenty-five feet or less.

POSITION OF THE UNION

Mr. Martin has served as a storekeeper for the company in another department for over three years and is completely familiar with and experienced in the job duties of storekeeper. The failure of employee Martin to qualify for the job in question may be attributed to two factors: first, the bias and discrimination exhibited by Foreman Oglethorpe in his handling of Martin's bid for the job; and secondly, Mr. Martin's alleged failures were directly the result of stumbling blocks put in his way by Foreman Oglethorpe and the employee about to be displaced.

Contrary to usual custom in the plant, employee Newman was retained on the departmental payroll throughout the entire trial period despite his displacement by the grievant. One can only conclude that Foreman Oglethorpe never intended that the grievant should get the job, otherwise the retention of Newman does not make sound economic sense. Further, at no point during the

grievant's trial period was he briefed in the duties of the job and
the manner in which these duties were to be undertaken by its
Foreman. Rather, Oglethorpe delegated this orientation to former
storekeeper Newman. His immediate dismissal from the job after
only a one-day trial, a dismissal corrected only after intervention
by higher company officials, evidences an attitude on the part of
Foreman Oglethorpe that the grievant would not be allowed to qualify.
Indeed, the sarcastic tone of the final quit notice further evidences
the bias of the foreman.

Since the company admits the job in question is a relatively
simple one, the only conclusion that can be drawn from the grievant's
failure to qualify is that stumbling blocks were put in his way. The
uncontradicted testimony of the grievant to the effect that he was
given the wrong "night list" destroys the evidentiary value of the
incident related by the company as to Martin's "hunting for hours
for dies which were already on the press." Further, the unrebutted
testimony of the witness to the effect that the stencilling of dies for
easy identification purposes had fallen into such a state of disuse
that only the foreman and employee Newman could locate them
easily. Since it is part of the storekeeper's job to see that all items
are properly stencilled for identification purposes, the failure of the
foreman to have Newman do so can only be interpreted as a conspi-
racy to protect his job.

The union requests that the arbitrator order a new trial period
for employee Martin, and that he be paid retroactively for all time
lost on layoff until he qualifies for the job of storekeeper in the main
press department.

Suggested Discussion Questions

(a) Does Article V, Section 13, guarantee to every employee the
    right to a trial period? If not, what criteria might be used to
    determine which employees are entitled to a trial? If no em-
    ployees are entitled to a trial period as a matter of contract
    right, what is the meaning of the clause in question?

(b) Would the contract language of Article V, Section 13, imply a
    different length of trial period for various employees? Explain.

(c) What criteria may be advanced for measuring whether an em-
    ployee has received a fair trial?

(d) What institutional difficulties were observable in both the
     company and union ranks which made the pursuance of their
     respective positions a rather delicate problem?

27. The Diamond Specialty Company Case

BACKGROUND OF THE CASE

On October 26, 1962, the company posted a notice of layoff to
take effect at the close of business on November 2, 1962. On
November 1, 1962, the company cancelled the scheduled layoff of
Mr. Carl Adams, a group leader, on the grounds that his expertise
was needed to prepare for the introduction of a new order which was
imminent. When the new order did not materialize, Mr. Adams was
given a layoff notice on November 13, 1962, and was laid off on
November 20, 1962.

The union grieved that the retention of Group Leader Adams,
while more senior operators were on layoff, violated the seniority
provisions of the agreement. The company denied this claim, and
the matter went to arbitration.

APPLICABLE CONTRACT PROVISIONS

Article XII

5. Where skill and ability are comparatively equal,
    seniority shall be the determining factor for purpose
    of layoffs for indefinite periods and discharges for
    lack of work deemed by the Company to be permanent.
    Rehiring of employees so discharged and recalls of
    employees so laid off shall be made from the waiting
    list hereinafter referred to on the same basis as such
    layoffs and discharges. The departments are as
    follows: (a) Maintenance; (b) Production; (c) Ware-
    house; and (d) Laboratory and Inspection Department.
    Departments listed as (a), (b), and (c) above shall be
    considered to be one unit in determining layoffs and
    recalls with respect to any employee affected who has

seniority of six (6) months or more. All employees
shall receive one week's notice of layoff.

6. Plant layoff lists will be maintained by departmental
   seniority.

Article XIV

2. The temporary or permanent use of group leaders
   shall rest solely in the judgment of management.

POSITION OF THE COMPANY

The company contends that failure to retain Mr. Adams would
inevitably have occasioned the company to promote or "upwardly
bump" whichever operator had remained in Group Leader Adams'
stead to the classification of group leader. But to promote any
more senior employee under these circumstances, the company
points out, would be contrary to the provisions of Article XII,
Section 5 of the agreement, would be contrary to the practice of
the parties, and contrary to the general rule of arbitration law.

The provisions of Article XII, Section 5 recognize two separate
classifications of employees, group leaders and operators, and
layoffs may be effected through consideration of the seniority of the
employee within his respective classification. Thus, the company
may carry out its reduction in force by applying the seniority rights
within each classification even though such action may result in the
retention of a group leader junior in plant seniority to an operator.
The retention of employee Adams, the company urges, was the
ordinary result of applying the seniority provisions to these separate
classifications.

Employee Adams had demonstrably superior ability over that
of any other employee for the work which the company expected him
to be performing. The specific work for which Mr. Adams was retained to perform was the preparation of the XQR area for the production of Nevis, a product for which the company expected to receive an important order in the immediate future. This anticipated
order would have been the largest ever received for a product and
would have provided employment for thirty-three employees in the
XQR area for a period exceeding 240 days.

Preparation included cleaning the equipment, changing over the equipment to accomodate the packaging of a new product, and making sure the equipment was in top order and ready to operate. With respect to this work, employee Adams was by far the more experienced, not only by virtue of his assignment as group leader in the XQR area, but because he had made the trial runs on this product several weeks previously. He also was completely familiar with the new packaging machinery and special mixing equipment which had been installed in the area. Although this order unfortunately failed to develop and Mr. Adams' skills were not needed, the company points out that as soon as the company received notice of the cancellation of the Nevis order, it immediately gave Mr. Adams a layoff notice of one week according to the contract provisions.

POSITION OF THE UNION

The practice of the parties has been to treat group leaders identically to operators at time of layoff. Whenever in the past a layoff occurred, group leaders would depart in order of seniority and were not given any special consideration by virtue of their position as group leaders. This practice has been in complete accord with the clear and unambiguous contract language which provides for layoff by departmental seniority rather than by classification. The job of group leader is a temporary position in the eyes of the company and can be awarded and retracted at whim. The company is wont to move a man back and forth between the job titles of operator and group leader. It is, therefore, no surprise that group leaders have always left the plant during layoffs in accordance with seniority based upon the same seniority list which includes operators. Indeed, there is no separate seniority list for group leaders.

The decision to retain Mr. Adams was based on the hoped-for order to produce a new formula (Nevis) for a principal customer. Receipt of this order would have required the preparation of certain machinery and equipment. But the length of time required to prepare the machinery and equipment was only two days from the time the order arrived. Thus, the company retained Mr. Adams while his seniors were being laid off because it believed he would be useful in a contingent happening. The usefulness would run for a period not in excess of two days. Because of these minimal and contingent factors, Mr. Adams worked between November 2, 1962 and November

20, 1962. The union urges that what Mr. Adams would have done
had the order arrived is of no importance; it is what he did during
the layoff which is of consequence.

The work done by Mr. Adams during the period of time in
question was primarily work of an operator which could have been
done and should have been done by the most senior employee on
layoff. But even assuming that the work done by him was "group
leader" work, it was work unrelated to his alleged expertise. This
expertise was never used. Instead, he performed work outside his
special area of ability—work that could have been performed by any
of those on layoff.

Even when his services were obviously not needed because of
the cancellation of the Nevis order, Mr. Adams was retained an
additional week while other employees more senior to him were on
layoff. The company seeks to justify this period of his employment
on the grounds of the one-week advance notice provision contained
in Article XII, Section 5 of the contract. The union submits that
the retention of Mr. Adams in the first place was improper and
that the company cannot mitigate its error by using the one-week
rule to justify keeping him under the circumstances. Since his employment out of seniority order during layoff was improper, this
error should have been corrected by an immediate layoff.

Suggested Discussion Questions

(a) What influence should the imminency of the special order have
in determining the right of the company to employ Mr. Adams
out of seniority order on the grounds of his "special-purpose"
ability?

(b) Should the decision as to the correctness of the company's
action, in effect, be dependent upon whether he carried out the
work which required his particular talents?

(c) What changes, if any, would the duration of this special-purpose
work introduce into the decision?

(d) Does the fact that the company has the unrestricted right in the
agreement to appoint and reject group leaders influence your
decision in determining the proper seniority unit?

28. The Excelsior Corporation Case

BACKGROUND OF THE CASE

The maintenance department in the Willington Plant of the company consists of five hourly paid employees who are supervised by a salaried foreman. The classifications and rates of pay of these employees are as follows:

Maintenance leader	$3.00
Maintenance machinist	3.00
Maintenance electrician and mechanic	3.00
Oiler and stitcher mechanic	2.73
General maintenance	2.69

On June 7, 1964, the company posted a temporary job of general maintenance man for bids in accordance with the contract.

Three employees bid for the job. They were, in order of their respective plant-wide seniority dates:

> Wilbert Baker—6/22/36
> Edward Clark—3/29/37
> Jack Dodds   —2/21/41

The company awarded the job to Mr. Dodds, and he worked in that classification from June 13, 1964 to August 15, 1964.

Mr. Baker filed a grievance claiming that his contractual seniority rights had been violated. The company denied the claim and the matter went to arbitration.

APPLICABLE CONTRACT PROVISIONS

Article IX

1. . . . Selection shall be made by the Company on the basis of qualifications and capability for the job, and when applicants are equally fit, plant seniority shall prevail. . . .

3. When a job of a temporary nature has to be filled, such job shall be filled in accordance with the provisions of Section 1 of this Article.

Article XX

This contract contains the entire agreement between the parties. In the event the Company and the Union agree to change or amend this contract, such change or amendment will be reduced to writing, dated, and signed by the parties and thereafter become a part of this Agreement.

POSITION OF THE COMPANY

Under the agreement the relative seniority of candidates for promotion to temporary vacancies becomes determinative only when the qualifications and capabilities of the candidates are equal. The issue is not whether the grievant, Mr. Baker, was qualified but rather whether he was as qualified as Mr. Dodds, the junior employee. Mr. Dodds had worked for more than six years in the maintenance department, whereas the grievant had never worked in that department. Mr. Dodds knew the work and was familiar with correct shop practice.

The work required included cleaning and painting; wiring and installation of electric fixtures; filling in a door; installing a window and exhaust system; tearing down and reinstalling a pipe rack; and functioning also as a general maintenance employee throughout the plant, working under general supervision but not under direct guidance. The skills and knowledge needed included painting, electrical work, carpentry, sheet metal work including torch burning, and general machine repair.

The work experience of the grievant, Mr. Baker, was clearly less than that of Mr. Dodds. As a production employee he made minor repairs to his machinery, but this is not experience within the preview of work done by the maintenance department which handles major repairs. Experience gained by Mr. Baker at other plants and as an independent contractor on his own time cannot be equated with plant experience. Only over the latter range of experience does the company have real knowledge of how well an employee carries out a job. Machines and methods differ from one plant to another and from industrial plants to the various com-

mercial situations in which employees might be engaged outside
working hours.

In a previous arbitration case dated February 14, 1962, Arbitrator C. J. Long upheld an identical selection of Mr. Dodds over
Mr. Baker for the job of general maintenance man. No significant
change in the seniority provisions of the agreement has since occurred. Indeed, the current agreement contains language with regard to the filling of temporary vacancies identical to the 1962 agreement language with regard to the filling of permanent openings.
Since the issue in 1962 was that of a permanent opening and the instant issue is that of a temporary opening, the same language is
controlling. Further, Mr. Dodds has occupied the post temporarily
on at least three occasions since then.

No agreement or common practice exists between the parties
to give the senior candidate a trial period on a given job, or to
teach the senior candidate the job in question. Further, practices
counter to the express provisions of Article IX have no validity
under the provisions of Article XX. During 1964 contract negotiations the union attempted to eliminate the contract requirement
that promotions shall be made upon the primary consideration of
qualifications and capability. The company refused to accede to
this demand. The union now is attempting to achieve through the
grievance procedure what it has been denied in negotiations.

POSITION OF THE UNION

The job in question is the lowest classification in the maintenance
department and the entry point into the maintenance department for
employees working in production jobs. The grievant was as qualified
as anyone else for this type of work and since he was the senior employee he should have been awarded the job.

The company in this instance predetermined who would get the
job opening on the basis of personal records. There was no inter-
view, no discussion with the respective applicants to determine the
full range of their respective capabilities. The union does not consider skill previously developed within a given department of the
company as the sole determinant of ability for a later job opening.
Yet this was the sole basis on which the company awarded the job
giving rise to the instant grievance.

Mr. Baker had gained the necessary experience both through

his past work history with the company and through outside work, with the result that for the job in question he was equally fit. He has carried out maintenance and repair work on papermaking machines, such as the changing of rolls, belts, and cylinders. He has repaired belts and pumps. He had helped in the tearing down and remodeling of the wet end of the papermaking machine, and has helped in the set-up of beater equipment. He has helped in the installation of new trusses and a new roof in the paper mill, as well as carried out considerable painting. Since the discontinuance of the paper mill and the resultant transfer of Mr. Baker to the box shop, he has gained a familiarity with its machinery and has fixed belts, changed saw blades, set up presses, and carried out miscellaneous minor repairs in the shop.

During his hours away from the plant he has gained experience in a wide variety of different maintenance skills. He has worked as a carpenter, an automotive mechanic, a truck driver, a painter, an electrician, and a paperhanger. He has done general construction work, concrete work, roofing and siding work, sheet metal work, among other outside occupations.

A well-established practice has been to allow employees a thirty-day trial period to prove their qualifications for promotion opportunity. While the union did attempt to limit the company's exercise of selection rights based on qualifications and ability at the last negotiation sessions, it did so in order to prevent the very abuse of such rights as is evidenced in the instant situation.

Suggested Discussion Questions

(a) To what extent, if at all, should the arbitrator in this case be guided by the decision of a prior arbitrator to the relative capabilities of Mr. Baker and Mr. Dodds?

(b) Do the provisions of Article XX eliminate from consideration all past practices with respect to the seniority rights of employees?

(c) Evaluate experience as a criterion of ability in the instant situation carefully, drawing a distinction between experience gained in the plant and that gained elsewhere.

(d) To what extent, if at all, should the company's failure to con-

sider the full range of Mr. Baker's ability through a procedural
error change the result if the arbitrator is convinced that the
placement of Mr. Dodds, though made arbitrarily, was nevertheless the proper choice under the agreement?

29. The Quinlan Company Case

BACKGROUND OF THE CASE

Labor grades within the company are classified in reverse
numerical order, the higher-ranking jobs bearing the lower numerical classifications. Labor grades within the regulator repair
department range from a low of labor grade nine to a high of labor
grade four. Within the heat treating department and the shipping
department the range is from labor grade twelve to labor grade five
and from labor grade twelve to labor grade seven respectively.

The company posted a vacant job in labor grade nine in the
regulator repair department. No employee within that department
bid for the job. Mr. Camper who was employed in a labor grade
ten job in the heat treating department and Mr. Davis who was employed in a labor grade nine job in the shipping department both bid
for the vacant job. The company awarded it to Mr. Camper, whereupon Mr. Davis filed the following grievance.

> I was improperly denied the job in labor grade nine
> in the Regulator Repair Department for which I bid. I
> have greater plant-wide seniority than Mr. Camper,
> and I also have the ability to perform the work of the
> posted job.

Unable to adjust the grievance to its satisfaction, the union processed the grievance to arbitration.

APPLICABLE CONTRACT PROVISIONS

Section 10—Promotions

10.3—Where a vacancy occurs in the bargaining unit
which constitutes an opportunity for a promotion, the

vacancy shall be posted throughout the plant for four (4)
working days, and then offered to an applicant presently
working in the department who has the longest continuous
service, provided he has the necessary qualifications to
perform the work. In the event that such a vacancy cannot be filled from within the department, the vacancy shall
be offered to someone in the bargaining unit, and the same
conditions of continuous service and qualifications shall
apply. If no applicant in the bargaining unit has the necessary qualifications to perform the work, the COMPANY,
at its discretion, can offer the opportunity to any employee
on a trial basis not to exceed sixty (60) days of actual
work; or hire a new man with the required experience.

* * *

10. 4—In the event of discontinuance of any group or
department, or where employees are displaced because
of technological changes, those employees shall be given
plant-wide seniority for the single purpose of qualifying
for a job, provided they have the ability to qualify, and
do qualify within a period of sixty (60) days of actual
work. Employees exercising their seniority under this
Section can claim any job in the plant held by an employee
of lower seniority in a like, or lower classification.
When transferring from one department to another department under this clause, the employee's total seniority shall be transferred to the new department immediately. Employees displaced by more senior employees, exercising their seniority under this Section,
shall exercise their seniority rights under all other
Sections of this AGREEMENT, except this Section.

POSITION OF THE UNION

Since the job in question is at the bottom of the promotional
ladder in the regulator repair department is scaled to greater heights
(labor grade four) than the promotional ladder in the shipping department (labor grade seven), the job in question offered a bona fide
promotional opportunity for the grievant. A promotion means a
"chance to advance" and/or a "preferment." The job in question

clearly gives the grievant an opportunity for increased advancement
over the promotional opportunities within his own department.

Under the language of Section 10.3 of the agreement the vacancy
need not result in an immediate promotion but may merely "constitute an opportunity for promotion." Since no employee within the
regulator repair department bid for the job in question, Section 10.3
provides that it "shall be offered to someone in the bargaining unit,
and the same conditions of continuous service and qualifications
shall apply." These conditions are likewise defined by Section 10.3
as the applicant "who has the longest continuous service provided he
has the necessary qualifications to perform the work." Mr. Davis
has the longest continuous service, and his qualifications have at
no point been questioned by the company. Therefore, he should be
awarded the job.

POSITION OF THE COMPANY

Under Section 10.3 of the agreement, bidding for job vacancies
is limited to those which constitute a promotion and does not en-
compass lateral transfers. A promotion is where an employee
moves up from one labor grade to another, and does not include a
lateral movement at the same job grade level. This section of the
agreement applies to vacancies giving rise to promotions, not
potential promotions. A promotion cannot be defined as "a chance
to advance" as the union contends, but rather it is defined as "to
exalt, to raise, to prefer, to advance." Obviously, none of these
meanings covers a lateral transfer.

During the 1962 negotiations the union attempted to change the
first sentence of Section 10.3 to read:

> When a vacancy occurs in the bargaining unit, the vacancy
> shall be posted throughout the plant for four (4) working
> days, and then offered to an applicant presently working
> in the department who has the longest continuous service,
> provided he has the necessary qualifications to perform
> the work.

The company refused to agree to these changes, and they were
dropped by the union. Thus, the union knew that employees did
not have the right to make lateral transfers and attempted to a-
chieve that right for them. But the company refused to grant such
a right.

Further, under the provisions of Section 10.4 of the agreement, lateral transfers are granted to employees where the discontinuance of a work group or department occurs. Therefore, as is apparent, the parties knew how to write a clause to provide for lateral transfers, but did not choose to do so in Section 10.3 of the agreement.

The company cannot afford to train an employee for a job in one labor grade and then permit him to transfer to a job in a similar labor grade either within the same department or in another department. The company, therefore, sought protection against this kind of move in the provisions of Section 10.3.

Suggested Discussion Questions

(a) What is meant by a "promotion"? To what extent does your definition resolve the instant issue?

(b) Why should the company so strenuously oppose lateral transfers?

(c) If a decision were rendered in favor of the union, how could it be worded so as to give the company considerable protection against its fear of lateral transfers?

(d) Of what significance is the 1962 bargaining history insofar as the determination of this case is concerned?

Bibliography

Healy, James J., "The Ability Factor in Labor Relations," Arbitration Journal, Vol. X, No. 6 (1955), pp. 3-11.

Horlacher, J. P., "Employee Job Rights versus Employer Job Control: The Arbitrator's Choice," Collective Bargaining and the Arbitrator's Role, Proceedings of the Fifteenth Annual Meeting, National Academy of Arbitrators, Pittsburgh, Pa., January 24-26, 1962 (Washington, D. C.: Bureau of National Affairs, 1962), pp. 165-196.

Howard, Wayne E., "Criteria of Ability," Arbitration Journal, Vol. XIII, No. 4 (1958), pp. 179-196.

_____, "Determination of Ability," Arbitration Journal, Vol. XII, No. 1 (1957), pp. 14-27.

_____, "Seniority Rights and Trial Periods," Arbitration Journal, Vol. XV, No. 2 (1960), pp. 51-64.

_____, "The Interpretation of Ability by Labor-Management Arbitration," Arbitration Journal, Vol. XIV, No. 3 (1959), pp. 117-132.

Sayles, Leonard R., "Seniority: An Internal Union Problem," Harvard Business Review, Vol. XXX, No. 1 (January-February, 1952), pp. 55-65.

Stone, Morris, Labor-Management Contracts at Work (New York: Harper & Row, Publishers, 1961), chap. iii, "Seniority and Ability," pp. 35-53.

Taylor, G. W., "Seniority Concepts," Arbitration Today, Proceedings of the Eighth Annual Meeting, National Academy of Arbitrators, Boston, Mass., January 27-28, 1955 (Washington, D. C.: Bureau of National Affairs, 1955), pp. 127-138.

CHAPTER 8

Distribution of Overtime

Most collective bargaining agreements provide for premium pay when employees work for periods in excess of eight hours per day or in excess of five days per week. These premium rates were originally conceived as penalty rates assessed against the employer for the over-utilization of his existing labor force. From a broad economic point of view their purpose was to spread the work and contribute to fuller employment, a view espoused not only by public and union officials, but by the employees, themselves, during the precarious days of mass unemployment prior to World War II, the period during which most of these clauses developed. Viewed more narrowly at the plant level, the deterrent aspects of these clauses were uppermost in the minds of management and labor bargainers, the idea essentially being one of preventing management for reasons of its own convenience from assigning work schedules deemed onerous or inconvenient to the employee. From the employee's viewpoint, it was thought to be essentially an equitable remedy for less desirable or more onerous working conditions.

The increase in the length of the work week during World War II and the increased overtime opportunities in the more prosperous post-war era, however, have changed the viewpoint of most employees towards overtime work to that of a positive working benefit because of the greatly enlarged opportunities of increasing income through the acceptance of premium pay overtime work assignments. Worker reluctance to work overtime, in more cases than not, has been converted to worker demand for an equitable division of overtime work opportunity.

While most collective bargaining agreements provide for some method of allocating overtime work opportunity on an equitable basis, the manner in which this is carried out varies widely. This often reflects the relative difficulties in the allocation process among different plants or even among different departments in the same plant. It also, like seniority issues, reflects the differing desires of workers with respect to their concept of equality in overtime work opportunity. Some agreements merely express a broad policy statement that overtime opportunities "will be spread as equally as possible," such policy being implemented by specific procedures and systems which vary as between work groups; other agreements include a long detailed procedure in the bargaining agreement itself.

Resolution of these issues involves the arbitrator in questions of both fact and contract interpretation. Was the work in question truly an overtime work opportunity? If so, under the particular procedure in effect who would be entitled to that work opportunity? Under what conditions is the company entitled to depart from the accepted procedure, and were these conditions controlling at the time of the alleged violation?

Frequently the parties are more concerned with the question of the proper remedy than with the question of whether there has been a contract violation. Management invariably argues that a substitute overtime work opportunity be made available to the employee who was overlooked or bypassed; the union invariably argues for a monetary remedy. This raises the basic question of how an overlooked employee can be "made whole," since the process of arbitration is one of equitable rather than punitive remedies. The question can become quite complex since it is dependent upon the specific procedure used and the amount of overtime work opportunity normally generated in the work unit for allocation.

CASES

30. The Bonita Company Case

BACKGROUND OF THE CASE

Mr. William J. Sloan is employed as a towmotor operator in the shipping and receiving department of the company. This department has been frequently assigned overtime Saturday work and often used employees from other departments of the plant. Problems over the distribution of this work had been many in the past, and the company agreed that to reduce potential sources of disputes in the future it would post notices of all weekend work opportunity in the department no later than Friday morning of that week.

On Friday, January 2, 1959, Mr. Sloan felt ill and at noon of that day asked to be excused to visit his family doctor. The excuse was granted. No notices had been posted for overtime Saturday work on January 3rd. Mr. Sloan asked his supervisor whether there would be work on January 3rd, and allegedly the supervisor replied, "Definitely not." Mr. Sloan then asked his lead man to get in touch with him should work for January 3rd develop.

When Mr. Sloan returned to work on Monday, January 5th, he discovered that the shipping and receiving department had worked overtime on Saturday, January 3rd and on Sunday, January 4th. He grieved that he was unfairly deprived of overtime work opportunity on Saturday, January 3rd. The parties were unable to adjust satisfactorily this grievance, and the union filed a demand for arbitration.

APPLICABLE CONTRACT PROVISIONS

Article 8—Overtime

6. All overtime shall be distributed on a departmental basis among qualified employees of that department.

POSITION OF THE UNION

When the company called in the whole shipping and receiving department on Saturday, January 3, 1959, without notifying Mr. Sloan, and further when employees of other departments were called in to perform work in that department on the day in question, Mr. Sloan's contract rights were violated.

The custom and practice has been for the company to post overtime weekend work schedules no later than the Friday morning preceding the weekend in question. The union has insisted at numerous grievance meetings that the practice of posting weekend schedules be adhered to, and the company has agreed to do so. Had the schedule been properly posted, the grievant would have been aware of the overtime work opportunity and would have been able to avail himself of it.

No definitive evidence was presented that the overtime work was of an emergency nature. On the contrary, the testimony indicated that at least a part of the work was carried out purely for inventory purposes. On many occasions the company has called employees from their homes to notify them of overtime work opportunity. There is little justification for its failure to do so in this instance.

The grievant was willing to accept overtime work. He had never before refused an overtime assignment, yet he worked in a department which is frequently assigned overtime work. The grievant further took the precaution of asking his supervisor about scheduled overtime work on Saturday before he was excused from the plant. He specifically requested that he be notified should such work develop. The company was under an obligation to notify him of the overtime work opportunity, and failing to do so, should reimburse him for the work opportunity which he missed.

POSITION OF THE COMPANY

Subsequent to Mr. Sloan's leaving of the plant on Friday for personal reasons, a customer's requirements necessitated emergency overtime work in the shipping and receiving department. Under these circumstances, where there has been no formal notification of overtime work and where an employee has absented himself from the plant for personal reasons, the company is under no obligation to call such absentee employee and advise him of over-

time work opportunity. The company points to the fact that in the
past it has never communicated with absentee employees for the
purpose of informing them of overtime work opportunity.

Suggested Discussion Questions

(a) The company claims that the work in question was emergency
work, while the union contends the work was merely unplanned.
In general, how would you distinguish between these two categories?

(b) What was the intent of the parties' agreement on the procedure
that the company would post weekend work schedules? What
obligation, if any, does the company assume for failure to post?

(c) Is the position of the grievant stronger because of the fact that
employees from other departments of the plant were used?
Explain.

(d) The company bases its case largely on the proposition that the
company has no obligation to notify or call in an absentee employee and never in the past has done so. Do you think a decision for the union in the instant situation will tend to upset
the accommodations the parties have already made with respect to the practice of not notifying an absentee employee?
Explain.

31. The Waterloo Corporation Case

BACKGROUND OF THE CASE

The union and the company experienced a long strike during the
summer and early fall of 1963. In settlement of that strike a memorandum of agreement was executed on October 3, 1963. The memorandum of agreement amended certain specific contract terms and,
in addition, included a memorandum of understanding regarding the
utilization of manpower. The memorandum of understanding reads:

> The Company has stated that it must have flexibility in
> order to make full utilization of manpower. This is
> necessary in order that the Company may stay in busi-
> ness and be competitive.

The Union representatives agree that the UNION and the employees will cooperate with the Company in order to bring this about.

The Union and employer representatives have engaged in long discussions of their intent and the following are some examples of the Company and Union expression of intent to bring this about.

1. The Union intends to cooperate with the Company in reassigning employees to get over jam-ups, emergency situations, and the like.
2. The Union recognizes that the Company shall make every effort to stop waste of manpower and that to this end it may have to combine jobs and take other reasonable and necessary measures.
3. The Union has told the stewards it does not want work stoppages and will tell the people that the Company intends to take disciplinary action against any individual or group advocating such action.
4. It is not the intent of the Company to use temporary transfers as a device to prevent people being recalled from layoff.
5. It is not the intent of the Company to put an employee on a job that he cannot do with intent to discharge him on the basis of lack of ability.
6. It is the intent of the Company that employees temporarily transferred will continue to accrue seniority in their own department.
7. It is not the intent of the Company to transfer employees from their own jobs and have other employees do their work.
8. It is not the intent of the Company to have employees do jobs that would be degrading.
9. The Company agrees that an employee who is temporarily doing work out of his classification shall be paid either the rate for the job on which he is working or his own rate, whichever is higher.

In substance, this understanding was sought by the company in order to regain certain rights in the utilization of its manpower. These rights, for the most part, had become eroded by contrary work practices which had grown up over an extended period of time,

an interim which spanned the duration of a number of collective bargaining agreements.

The union and the company cannot agree on the intent, interpretation, and application of this memorandum with respect to the
factual situations contained in a number of grievances, of which the
following issue is one.

Prior to the time of the strike, as well as after the strike, the
ice plant was operated on a seven-day week schedule. From time
to time there would be no ice packing work to do, and these employees would be then temporarily assigned to the cylinder platform
in the ice plant to fill out their day.

On Sunday, October 20, 1963, the railroad box car in which
dry ice is shipped did not arrive and there was, consequently, no
work for the three employees in question to perform at that location.
In order to utilize their time they were assigned to performing work
in the B. & D. department. In the morning they filled some drums,
and in the afternoon they did some stencilling work. The rate of pay
for ice packers is $2.12 per hour, but for the entire day in question
they were paid at the rate of $2.34 per hour, which is an operator's
rate of pay in the B. & D. department. The stencilling work which
was performed in the afternoon normally pays $2.10 per hour.

POSITION OF THE UNION

Since the ice plant is on a seven-day schedule and Sunday is a
part of the regularly scheduled work week, where B. & D. is on a
five-day schedule and Sunday is a double-time day, the work performed by ice packers in the B. & D. department represented overtime work in that department which was performed by ice packers
at the straight-time B. & D. rate. The established practice has
always been to assign overtime work in a department to the employees of that department, and the company has never suggested
or requested that the practice be changed.

The memorandum of understanding does not contemplate the
use of temporary transfers to avoid the payment of weekend overtime either expressly or by implication. The company did not con-
sult with the union when it unilaterally departed from the established
practice, yet the memorandum speaks of the term "cooperation"
which embodies the concept of mutual agreement.

Since the transfer was made in violation of the established
practice respecting the assignment of overtime work opportunity,

and in violation of the memorandum of understanding, the company should be required to compensate the B. & D. employees at double time for the overtime work in that department performed by the three ice packers.

POSITION OF THE COMPANY

In view of the entire background, including an extended strike and lengthy negotiations, which resulted in the reduction to writing of very broad language expressing the intention of the parties to permit the company to utilize fully its manpower and specifically stating what was going to happen when an employee was temporarily transferred to another department, it is difficult to accept the union interpretation that the company has no right to transfer across departmental lines. If the right were restricted, as the union contends, such restrictions would have been spelled out in the agreement. If the union were to be successful in its contention in this case, then it can be anticipated that it would argue that whenever employees are temporarily assigned to perform work which is normally performed by other employees, the latter employees are being deprived of an opportunity to perform such work on an overtime basis and therefore the assignment is improper. It is not difficult to see what such a construction could do to the flexibility which was secured by the company in the memorandum of understanding.

The work in question should not be considered overtime work because it was a regular work day for the employees who performed the work. It was not overtime work but merely fill-in work. The work could have been done in the normal course of events the following week by the employees of the B. & D. department. Even if it is considered to be in a sense overtime work, the company's right to utilize fully and to avoid the waste of manpower should not be restricted. While it is true that there was no discussion during the negotiations of the specific question of Sunday work, a reading of the language, as well as the entire background leading up to the creation of the memorandum supports the company's position in this issue. Men who had been called to work had idle time, and the company, in good faith, utilized their time to perform work which was available. This was done to avoid a waste of manpower. If the company had sent these men home it would, nevertheless, have been obligated to pay them their regular pay for eight hours.

Suggested Discussion Questions

(a) Suppose that there was work for the ice packers in their regular assignment, but during the course of that assignment, they were reassigned to B. & D. work for the purpose of relieving congestion in the latter department. Under these conditions do you think that the company would have committed a violation?

(b) Although the company's "broad rights to gain flexibility in the use of manpower" included certain express limitations spelled out in the memorandum of understanding, the memorandum contained no restriction against using temporary transfers to dilute overtime work opportunity. Does this mean that the company is free to use temporary transfers for this purpose? Does it matter that the policy of equalization of overtime work opportunity was not established through contract language but through past work practices?

(c) Neither the company's nor the union's interpretation of what constitutes overtime work opportunity seems particularly persuasive. How would you distinguish between overtime work opportunity and fill-in work in this instance?

(d) During the hearing a company official bluntly stated that under the memorandum the company could assign ice packers "to any department which is short of help." Under the circumstances outlined above can it be said that the B. & D. department was short of help?

32. The Zenger Company Case

BACKGROUND OF THE CASE

The company operates on a three shift schedule: shift one works from 8 A. M. to 4 P. M. ; shift two from 4 P. M. to midnight; shift three from midnight until 8 A. M. On June 15, 1964 the company

found it necessary to schedule overtime on the third shift in order
to clean the heaters on a still. A mechanic, Mr. Joseph Lord, who
worked on the second shift, was held over to help with this work.
Mr. Thomas Armstrong, a mechanic helper on the first shift, filed
a grievance alleging that it was his turn to work the overtime.

Allegedly, the practice at the time of the incident was for the
employees themselves to keep track of their overtime. When overtime was scheduled, the foreman merely asked the group whose
turn it was to work overtime. On the day in question, the employees
were not asked, but the second-shift mechanic was assigned the
overtime work opportunity.

When Mr. Armstrong approached his foreman, Mr. Osler, on
the following morning about the denial of overtime work opportunity,
Mr. Osler admitted he made a mistake and offered Mr. Armstrong
overtime work opportunity on the following night. Mr. Armstrong
took the position that he should be compensated for improper denial
of overtime work opportunity and filed a grievance. Unable to adjust
this matter to its satisfaction, the union filed a demand for arbitration.

APPLICABLE CONTRACT PROVISIONS

Article 3—Overtime

1. Overtime in each department will be spread as equally
   as possible, subject to the ability of the employees to
   perform the available work.

POSITION OF THE UNION

The system of overtime distribution then in existence and ac-
quiesced in by the company was for employees to maintain their
own informal overtime schedule. Overtime was distributed by
selecting each man in turn on the informal list. If a man refused
overtime or was unavailable for work when his turn came around,
it would be treated as a turn worked, and the next person on the
list would receive the overtime. The company in the instant situation simply ignored this schedule and as a result violated Article
3, Section 1, of the agreement.

The factor of ability had nothing to do with the overtime assign-

ment. It could be done equally well by either a mechanic or a
mechanic helper. The assignment was scheduled before the shift
in question, and there was no impediment to following the informal
list. Foreman Osler admitted he made a mistake when notified of
the situation. There can be no clearer violation, innocent as it may
be. The dispute, therefore, from the outset concerned the proper
remedy.

In the one instance where a similar violation occurred in another
area of the plant, the company awarded a monetary remedy. No witness, either union or company, was aware of a situation in which the
mechanical forces had ever been worked out of turn. Many arbitration decisions also hold that an employee improperly denied overtime work opportunity is entitled to compensation for the hours which
he lost. The union, therefore, requests that the grievant be awarded
eight hours pay at time and one-half his hourly rate for the improper
denial of overtime work opportunity.

POSITION OF THE COMPANY

The agreement only requires overtime to be equalized, and the
company is not bound to follow the specific lists kept informally by
the employees. The union was unable to show that the company had
agreed to follow the lists, and since the subject of overtime assignment is specifically covered by Article III, any contrary practice
would not be binding. Although the grievant testified that the work
in question was "helper's work," Superintendent Singer testified
that on occasion the company used two mechanics for this work.
Further, in those cases reported where the issue has been raised,
arbitrators have consistently held that a company has the right to
select employees in any classification it chooses, in the absence of
a specific contractual provision to the contrary.

In cases involving similar facts, the weight of arbitral authority
holds that a contractual requirement to equalize overtime requires
that it only be done over a reasonable period of time. The company
supports this position with a list of cases.

Even if the assignment were improper, which the company denies,
there was no testimony showing a practice to pay for the improper
distribution of overtime opportunity. Witness Lyle could recall only
one such case, his own, which occurred in another department. Obviously, such an isolated instance under totally different circum-

stances cannot constitute practice or precedent. Further, other
arbitrators have upheld the offering of other than monetary remedies.

Suggested Discussion Questions

(a) Do you think the company is under any obligation to follow the
informal employee list? If not, what are its obligations?
Discuss fully.

(b) Was the company in a position under the existing system to
equalize overtime opportunity over reasonable periods of
time? If so, how could it accomplish this?

(c) This specific dispute evolved as part of a larger area of disagreement over work assignments, and considerable agrument
occurred on both sides as to which classification the work in
question really should be assigned. Should the arbitrator attempt to resolve this question before he grapples with the overtime assignment issue?

(d) Assume that you have decided for the union. What factors
would be most persuasive in determining whether future overtime opportunity or a monetary remedy is most appropriate?

33. The Young Company Case

BACKGROUND OF THE CASE

On Friday, February 19, 1965, Mr. Thomas Jackson, who was
employed by the company as a blanker, asked his foreman, Mr.
Ross, whether he would be permitted to work overtime on the following day. Mr. Ross replied that he would give Mr. Jackson his
answer before 4 P.M. on Friday, but that before giving him an
answer he wished to discuss with him his failure to report on three
previous Saturdays after having accepted overtime assignments on
those days. Mr. Jackson's excuses for having failed to report after
accepting an overtime assignment on the three previous occasions
were: sickness, car trouble, and hangover, respectively. Foreman
Ross attempted to locate Mr. Jackson at 3:55 P.M. on Friday, but

was unable to do so. He was not at his work station, nor had he come to the foreman's office as allegedly most employees do at the close of their shift.

The following week Mr. Jackson discovered that a less senior employee had been assigned the overtime work on Saturday, February 20, and this work had continued into Monday, February 22, a paid holiday under the agreement. Mr. Jackson then filed the following grievance:

> I, the undersigned, charge the company has violated past practice by not asking me to work overtime as the Senior man. I ask that I be made whole for all losses suffered.

Unable to resolve the dispute to its satisfaction, the union filed a demand for arbitration.

APPLICABLE CONTRACT PROVISIONS

Article 5—Overtime Work

2. No employee shall be discriminated against because of his inability to work overtime.

Article 27—Plant Rules

Violation of the following plant rules may result in discipline including discharge.

* * *

9. Repeated absenteeism and tardiness.

* * *

27. Failure to notify foreman when expected to be absent.

POSITION OF THE UNION

The general practice with respect to the distribution of overtime in the area wherein the grievant works is to offer it to the senior employee. As the senior employee, the grievant should have been assigned the overtime work.

During the grievance procedure the company admitted that the reason why the grievant was not given the overtime assignment was disciplinary in nature. It is a well-settled principle in arbitration that management may not deny contract benefits or rights for the purpose of administering discipline. If the company desires to discipline, it must do so directly, and not indirectly by withholding other benefits. The company has the power to discipline under the plant rules, particularly in the instant situation under Rule 9 and Rule 27.

The company cannot avoid its responsibility by the mere fact that Foreman Ross was unable to find the grievant at 3:55 P.M. Foreman Ross had an obligation to discuss the problem with the grievant before the very end of the working day, particularly on a holiday weekend.

The grievant should be made whole for all lost earnings, both on Saturday, February 20 and on Monday, February 22 at the premium rates applicable to those days.

POSITION OF THE COMPANY

On the three Saturdays preceding the incident in question the grievant accepted overtime assignments and failed to report. On the third occasion Foreman Ross warned him that if he failed to report he would not be asked again. Mr. Jackson failed to report and when questioned about his failure admitted he was suffering from a hangover.

No contractual provision exists regarding the assignment of overtime work opportunity. The company agreed in Article 5 that "no employee shall be discriminated against because of his inability to work overtime." This clause is not relevant since the grievant was not discriminated against for his inability to work overtime. The problem faced here is the grievant's repeated acceptance of overtime assignments and his failure to report to work.

Viewing the denial of overtime work opportunity as a disciplinary measure is a misconstruction of the company's action on the part of the union brought about largely through an admittedly poor choice of words on the part of the company at the grievance sessions. The denial of overtime work opportunity cannot be viewed as a punishment. The grievant was denied the opportunity because on repeated occasions he did not show up. The company must assign overtime work to employees on whom it can depend.

The rules cited by the union have only been applied to regularly

scheduled work days and not to weekend or holiday work. The
company has never disciplined for a failure to report on overtime
work days. Thus, it has no other means to discipline an employee
for failure to report on an overtime day. The company attempted
to explain the situation to the grievant on Friday, February 19, but
he could not be found. The grievant had an obligation to get this
matter resolved before he left the plant.

<u>Suggested Discussion Questions</u>

(a) The contract between the parties contains no provision relating
to the distribution of overtime work opportunity, and the alleged
violation is based on the fact that the company departed from its
customary practice in this respect. To what extent, if at all, is
a departure from practice different from a departure from a procedure contained in the agreement itself? Explain.

(b) Discuss the general principle of denial of contract benefits as a
form of disciplinary action. Are there any exceptions to the
principle as it was stated by the union?

(c) If you were the company attorney, how would you get away from
what the union has termed the "indirect discipline" character of
the company's action by the use of an alternative approach?

(d) As has often been stated, in arbitration proceedings the union
"may win the battle but lose the war." This may refer to the
fact that a decision in its favor may cause it more problems in
the future than a decision for the company. What aspects of
this case put it in that category?

34. The Xavier Company Case

BACKGROUND OF THE CASE

On October 9, 1963 the grievant, Mr. Thomas Connor, a
machinist employed in the machine shop of the Xavier Company,
was denied overtime work opportunity. At the time in question Mr.
Connor and two other machinists had an equal amount of overtime

hours charged against their work record. Under these circumstances the policy and practice of the company is to award the overtime work opportunity to the senior employee who was Mr. Connor.
Mr. Connor grieved the action of the company as follows:

> I was not scheduled to work overtime when it was my turn.
> I request the Company pay me 4 hrs. pay at the time and
> a half rate.

The company submitted the following answer to the grievance:

> In this case, on 9-9-63 two of the Machinists scheduled
> had the same amount of hours scheduled as Thomas Connor
> and by using good judgment I bypassed Connor for the fol-
> lowing reasons: (1) Connor was seriously ill for 16 weeks
> and came back to work Sept. 30. (2) On Saturday 10-5-63
> he was scheduled to work and declined. (3) The job assign-
> ment and hours (4:30 P.M. to 5:00 A.M.) were very strenu-
> ous, even for a man in his best condition. (4) I knew that
> Connor had to be scheduled the following Saturday, October
> 12, 1963. (He declined again.) Therefore grievance is
> denied.

The parties were unable to resolve this issue to the satisfaction of
the union and the union filed a demand for arbitration.

APPLICABLE CONTRACT PROVISIONS

Article 5—Scheduling and Recording of Overtime

13.   In the event that an employee has not been scheduled
      nor charged for a particular overtime assignment and
      files a grievance as a result of not being assigned over-
      time and the grievance terminates in the result that
      such aggrieved employee is paid for overtime not
      worked, such hours as are agreed to be paid will be
      charged against this employee's overtime schedule
      as well as against the schedule of the employee who
      was actually scheduled.

* * *

17.   If the Company desires to work a man overtime out
      of his regular turn for some exceptional reason, the

Foreman of the department in which the affected employees are members will contact the man who would
normally be scheduled to work and explain to such bypassed individual the situation involved and the reason
that he is being bypassed in favor of another employee,
and at the same time the man or men involved will be
assured by the Foreman that they will be given an opportunity to make up the amount of time, which was
not assigned, as soon as possible.

* * *

22. It is agreed that the Company has the right to schedule
overtime work. No employee shall be discriminated
against or disciplined for inability to work overtime.
Overtime will be distributed as equally as possible
within a classification except as affected by layoffs,
leaves of absence, sickness, and the like, but anyone
who is scheduled to work overtime and fails to work
or refuses to work, thereby forfeits that turn of participation in overtime work.

POSITION OF THE UNION

The action of the company in bypassing Mr. Connor violated
Paragraph 17 of Article 5 of the agreement. The foreman was
aware that Mr. Connor was first in line for overtime work opportunity, but deliberately bypassed him. The foreman not only drew
his own conclusions about whether the grievant should have been
given the overtime assignment, but failed to contact him and to explain the reasons why he was bypassed as Paragraph 17 requires.

The reasons given by the foreman for bypassing the grievant
without contacting or consulting him are insufficient. The mere
fact that Mr. Connor was out sick for some 16 weeks is no excuse.
Neither is the failure of Mr. Connor to work overtime on previous
occasions. Moreover, the work in question was the grievant's
regular work. If the grievant is physically able to carry out this
work on a regular basis, he is physically able to carry it out on an
overtime basis.

The equalization of overtime hours in the future is not a proper
remedy. While the union admits that the overtime of the grievant

has become equalized, this has been carried out through charging him with overtime hours on occasions when the grievant has refused weekend work opportunity. Mr. Connor has always refused overtime work opportunity on weekends. Therefore, he cannot be made whole for the denial of weekday overtime opportunity through an offer of weekend overtime work, an offer which the grievant will in all likelihood refuse, as he has in the past. The practice in the past has been to pay employees for lost overtime work opportunity when they have been improperly bypassed as evidenced in the settlement of three prior grievances identified as the Marshall, Zack, and Smith grievances.

POSITION OF THE COMPANY

Under the conditions prevailing at the time the instant issue arose, the foreman was entirely right in not assigning the grievant to the overtime work. The company points to the grievant's recent illness and the fact that the job in question was particularly arduous. The job consisted of tearing down a tube-sizing machine, an assignment which embodies heavy work. While the procedure employed by the foreman may have been contrary to company policy in that the individual concerned was not contacted, the decision was based on good judgment.

Nothing in the agreement or prior practice requires the company to pay for lost overtime opportunity, even if it results from an error on the part of the company. The overtime discrepancy was equalized very promptly, and the grievant has, therefore, been made whole. It is not contemplated that overtime shall be equalized hour by hour. Moreover, with few exceptions, the company does not pay for work that is not done.

The grievances referred to by the union do not indicate a policy or practice on the part of the company to pay for lost overtime work opportunity. While monetary remedies were applied to achieve settlement of each of these grievances, the language of the settlement terms makes clear that the settlements had no force in creating precedent. In the Marshall grievance, the settlement terms read: "This settlement is not precedent setting and is without prejudice." Likewise in the Zack grievance, the language of settlement terms states: "However, the settlement of this case shall not be construed as policy setting but based entirely on the merits of the individual case and will be settled without prejudice." The Smith grievance settlement terms provide: "The settlement of this grievance on the terms stated above shall not bind the company in future cases." For these reasons, the company urges that the grievance settlements put into evidence by the union are irrelevant.

Suggested Discussion Questions

(a) One of the difficulties in the company's position is that in its own mind it is convinced that the foreman was "entirely right" in a judgment call to bypass the grievant, yet it fails to sub-stantiate on an evidentiary basis the judgment of the foreman. As the company attorney or spokesman what evidence would you desire in order to make a more formidable case for the company?

(b) Suppose on the basis of the evidence, the arbitrator found that the company had proper grounds for bypassing the grievant, but nevertheless was guilty of a technical violation of not following contract procedures for notifying the grievant of the fact that he was to be bypassed. Would this make a difference in the remedy for violation?

(c) To what extent should an arbitrator take into consideration the specific language of grievance settlements when the language is at variance with the pattern of the settlements, themselves?

(d) Is the company argument on the remedy inconsistent with any of the contract provisions?

35. The Collingswood Company Case

BACKGROUND OF THE CASE

The company is a manufacturer of heavy machinery and normal-ly operates on a two-shift basis. The first shift begins at 7:00 A.M. and ends at 3:30 P.M. The second shift begins at 3:30 P.M. and ends at midnight. Because of a sudden influx of new orders, the company established a third shift in one department of the plant.

Most of the employees on the third shift were new employees, and
therefore the company preferred that the shift take over each work
day from the first and second shifts; for this reason the company
scheduled this shift from midnight to 7:00 A.M. starting on Monday
midnight. Thus, the fifth working day began on Friday at midnight
and ran to 7:00 A.M. on Saturday morning. The company paid employees their regular base rates for this work. Overtime work opportunity was frequent and ran from Saturday midnight until 7:00
A.M. on Sunday morning. For this work the company paid employees time and one-half their regular base rates for this overtime work.

The union filed a grievance contending that the Saturday work
performed by the third shift should be compensated at time and one-
half regular base rates and the Sunday overtime work should be
compensated at double regular base rates. Unable to resolve the
dispute to its satisfaction, the union filed a demand for arbitration.

APPLICABLE CONTRACT PROVISIONS

Article III—Hours and Overtime

Section 1
(a) The regular work week shall consist of forty (40)
hours, five (5) days from Monday to Friday inclusive,
consisting of eight (8) hours each day.

(b) Any changes in the regular work day and/or week
as referred to in Section 1(a) of this Article shall not be
made effective until mutually agreed to by both parties.

Section 2. All work performed in excess of eight (8)
hours in any single day, or in excess of forty (40) hours
in any week and all work performed on Saturdays shall
be paid at the rate of time and one-half.

Section 3. Doubletime shall be paid for all work performed on Sundays and recognized holidays.

POSITION OF THE UNION

Since the third shift begins on Monday at midnight, employees
on this shift on their fifth regularly scheduled day work from mid-

night Friday until 7:00 A. M. Saturday morning. Under the clear contract language of Article III, Section 2 of the agreement, these employees are entitled to premium pay for that portion of their schedule. By the same token any employee who reports to work at midnight on Saturday for overtime work should receive double time in accordance with the Sunday pay provisions contained in Article III, Section 3 of the agreement.

The day on which the work is performed is not determined by whether the shift is classified as first, second, or third, but rather the specific calendar day on which the work is performed. If the company desires to schedule its third shift from Tuesday at 12:01 A. M. through Saturday at 7:00 A. M., then it has an obligation to negotiate such an exception with the union. Failing to do this, it is liable for premium payments to all employees who actually worked on Saturday and Sunday in accordance with the contract provisions.

POSITION OF THE COMPANY

Article III, Section 1(a) of the agreement establishes a five-day week, Monday through Friday, and this must be taken into account in interpreting Section 2 or Section 3 of that Article. The whole shift structure begins on Monday with the first shift; thus the third shift on Monday must begin at midnight of Monday, otherwise the term "third" has no meaning. Thus, the Friday midnight shift must be considered Friday work, regardless of when it is performed.

If Section 2 or Section 3 of the agreement is read in a contrary fashion, it does violence to the clear language of Section 1. The agreement must be interpreted in such fashion as to make all the provisions consistent. The only manner in which this basic rule of contract interpretation can be effectuated in the instant situation is by the interpretation offered by the company.

Suggested Discussion Questions

(a) Suppose the disputed shift had been operating for some seven months before the union filed a grievance. What effect would this have on: (1) the arbitrability of the grievance; (2) the effect to be given to the seven months' practice on determining the merits of the dispute; and (3) the remedy which might be awarded.

(b) The company points out in a collateral argument that none of
     the third shift employees has complained of the shift scheduling.
     It concludes, therefore, that the union has no legitimate cause
     to complain, but merely wishes to harass the company. Do you
     agree with this reasoning? Explain.

(c) Suppose the company and the union had attempted at numerous
     meetings to negotiate an exception from the language of Article
     III, Section 1 for the third shift but failed to reach agreement.
     Do you think this strengthens or weakens the position of the
     company when the matter later comes to arbitration? Explain.

(d) Suppose Section 2 and Section 3 of Article III merely stated:

> All work performed in excess of eight (8) hours per
> day and forty (40) hours per week shall be paid at the
> rate of time and one-half.
> All work performed in excess of twelve (12) hours
> per day and forty-eight (48) hours per week shall be
> paid at doubletime rates.

     Would the company be in violation of the agreement, and if so,
     what would be the proper remedy?

Bibliography

Stone, Morris, Labor Management Contracts at Work (New York:
     Harper & Row, Publishers, 1961), chap. ix, "Overtime,"
     pp. 157-190.

CHAPTER 9

Subcontracting

Contracting out is the practice of arranging with another firm to make goods or perform services which conceivably could be performed by bargaining unit employees. Since even the largest of our business establishments are not self-sufficient and even the smallest must perform some work themselves, the question of making versus purchasing components, and performing services with bargaining unit employees versus purchasing these services from others are characteristic of the decision-making activities of large and small business alike.

Management usually regards the "make or buy" question as central to that body of decisions which might be termed strategic to the firm and is most reluctant to agree to limitations on its determinations of these matters. The union views such determinations, however, as threats to the bargaining unit and the job security of its members. Under these conditions disputes over subcontracting are likely to be argued in broad philosophical terms stretching beyond the narrow facts of the nature and type of work transferred.

Most collective bargaining agreements do not contain provisions on subcontracting. Management relies on this contract silence and the management rights clause in an effort to prove that its discretion in these matters is particularly broad, if not exclusive. The union argues that contract silence, even when combined with a strong management clause, cannot overcome the implied limitations on subcontracting which are contained in the recognition, seniority, job classification, and wage provisions of the agreement.

In applying the above principles to the facts of specific situations, arbitrators have applied much more pragmatic criteria to test the validity of management's action. Were the skills of bargaining unit employees and supervision sufficient to carry out the work at issue? Was the necessary equipment available? Could bargaining unit employees and company supervision have completed the disputed work within the scheduled time? Was it the type of work frequently subcontracted in that particular industry or by that particular company? Was the subcontracting one of permanent and continuing work or was it of a specific and unrepeated project? What was the impact of the subcontracting on the bargaining unit? Was it undertaken as a good faith business decision for sound business reasons, or was it an attempt to undercut the wage provisions of the agreement?

In the minority of agreements where express limitations are contained on subcontracting, the limitations range from a mere requirement for the company to inform and to discuss with the union proposed subcontracting to an outright prohibition on subcontracting work regularly carried out by bargaining unit employees. One intermediate limitation is that of reasonableness wherein the company agrees to make reasonable efforts to use its own manpower. Another, and perhaps the most common of the limiting provisions, is the prohibition of subcontracting when the firm's own employees are on layoff or when layoff or demotion of bargaining unit employees would result from the subcontracting.

In attempting to apply these provisions to the facts of a specific situation, arbitrators must grapple with such problems as: What is normal or regular bargaining unit work? What is reasonable effort on the part of the company? Did the subcontracting actually cause the reduction or layoff of a bargaining unit employee?

CASES

36. The Pennsylvania Company Case

BACKGROUND OF THE CASE

The company is a manufacturer of tubing. A part of the necessary tooling for each manufacture is mandrils. The company
formerly purchased these mandrils in the form of rough forgings
which were turned in the tool and die shop by the machine bench
operator. The rough forgings were purchased on terms of a given
price per pound. The vendor was not shipping the rough forgings
in precise dimensions, and the purchase of them in this form represented a material waste which was costly.   In an effort to get
more precise dimensions and to reduce the amount of steel purchased, the company began to purchase the material for mandrils
in the form of machine forgings ready for heat treatment. Along
with the material saving it reduced the turning time on the part of
the machine bench operator from six hours per mandril to approximately three hours per mandril.

Still later a vendor who had substantial unutilized capacity offered the company the material in a semi-finished state. The
company took advantage of this offer which reduced the turning
time by the machine bench operator still further to approximately
one hour per mandril.

During the spring of 1965 the company demoted three employees
who previously were classified as machine and bench operators in
the tool and die department to the classification of simple machine
operator, a classification which pays some 45 cents per hour less.
On May 1, 1965 the three employees grieved as follows:

> The below named employees are unjustly demoted. While
> work is being sent out to be done by outside contractors.
> We feel if the Company has work in these men's classifi-
> cations, they should be doing it.

The grievance was not settled in a manner satisfactory to the union, and it filed a demand for arbitration. During the hearing the parties jointly agreed that the issue to be arbitrated was:

Has the Company violated the Agreement by subcontracting work which subcontracting resulted in the downgrading of certain employees of the Tool and Die Department?

APPLICABLE CONTRACT PROVISIONS

Article 3—Direction of the Working Force

(1) Subject to the terms of this Agreement and any Supplemental thereto, the direction of the working force, including the right to assign work to employees, to require from every employee efficient utilization of his services, to promulgate and enforce plant rules and regulations, and to hire, suspend, promote, demote, transfer, discharge, or relieve employees from duty because of lack of work or for other legitimate reasons is vested exclusively with the Management of the DIVISION, provided that claims of discriminatory promotion or demotion and of wrongful or unjust discipline or discharge shall be subject to the grievance procedure herein provided.

(2) It is the intent of both parties to this Agreement to cooperate in eliminating grievances, waste, and inefficiency, and in effecting mill economies.

POSITION OF THE UNION

The company is presently subcontracting work which the grievants had previously performed in the tool and die department. Had the work not been sent out, the demotions for lack of work would not have been effected. Thus the action of the company is discrimination in demotion under the provisions of Article III of the agreement.

While the company has subcontracted work in the past without objection by the union, the work in question can be distinguished in several fundamental respects. First, the work in question represents a greater volume of subcontracting than had been carried out

in the past. Secondly, subcontracting in the past was never responsible for layoffs or demotions, but in the instant situation downgrades
were the direct result of the company's actions. Thirdly, on previous occasions the subcontracting was carried out because the work
force did not have the necessary skills to perform the work or because the company could not otherwise meet promised due dates; in
the instant situation, these factors are not present and normal every-
day work of the machine and bench operator is being subcontracted.

The union requests that the grievants should be made whole for
the company's improper action by awarding them the differences between the rates of pay of simple machine operator and that of machine
and bench operator, the classification they would have remained in,
had the company not improperly subcontracted the work in question.

POSITION OF THE COMPANY

Under the provisions of Article III of the agreement the company
has been vested with the exclusive right to manage including broad
rights over the direction of the working forces. Unless there is an
express restriction in the agreement against subcontracting, and
there is none, the company has the right to subcontract work. The
union has attempted in prior negotiations to restrict or limit the
company's rights in this regard, but the company has uniformly rejected these bargaining demands.

The company has always subcontracted die work in the plant,
and during this long history of subcontracting there have been numerous occasions of subcontracting while employees were on layoff or
which resulted in employees being downgraded. Where possible the
company has attempted to limit the subcontracting of dies to outside
vendors when the volume of work in its own shop is low, but it cannot agree to do this as a matter of contract, or to abide by such a
policy under all circumstances.

The decision to subcontract was a reasonable business decision.
It was not made arbitrarily, discriminatorily, or capriciously, nor
did it result from any desire to weaken the bargaining unit. The decision made by the company to purchase mandrils in a semi-finished
state is not a subcontracting issue in the normal sense of the term.
The real savings involved in the purchase of raw material in a new
and different form, though more highly finished, was considerable,
and the company would have been derelict in its responsibilities if
it had not taken advantage of this offer.

The action of the company cannot by any stretch of the imagination be deemed a discriminatory demotion. There was no discrimination against any of the employees involved. The demotion was for lack of work, and the employees are properly paid for the work to which they are now assigned.

Suggested Discussion Questions

(a) Is the union charge of discrimination under Section III of the Agreement well taken? Explain. On what other basis might the union contest the company's action?

(b) The company seeks to justify its subcontracting of mandrils on the basis of its prior history of die subcontracting. To what extent, if at all, should its practice with respect to the subcontracting of dies control its rights to subcontract mandrils? Explain.

(c) Of what relevance is the fact that in the present circumstances the subcontracting of mandrils was directly responsible for the downgrading of employees? Would your answer be the same if the agreement contained a clause providing that "no subcontracting will be undertaken by the company while employees are on layoff"?

37. The Quaker Company Case

BACKGROUND OF THE CASE

The company, a pharmaceutical manufacturer, maintains an experimental farm in order to test animal health products developed in the laboratory. Among the animals raised are sheep of which there are currently some 200. For identification purposes each sheep at birth receives a number which is placed on a metal tag inserted in its ear. The number is then stamped in ink upon the sheep in order that it may be identified at a distance. Periodically the number must be restamped on the sheep as the number becomes difficult to read with the wearing off of the ink and the natural growth of the wool. Bargaining unit employees performed this stamping operation as a routine part of their work since the organization of their bargaining unit in 1958.

Sheep are sheared annually, and the custom at the farm has been to carry out this operation early in the spring so that the wool may be sold at the annual wool sale held in the area during the early part of June. Sheep shearing is a skilled trade. Because of the limited number of sheep raised in the area, the only available shearers are a few persons who do it on a part-time basis. There is not enough work in the area to support a man as a full-time sheep shearer. When sheep are sheared, it is necessary to restamp them for identification purposes.

From 1958 or 1959 through 1963 the company utilized the services of a student at a nearby university on a part-time basis to carry out the shearing operation on an independent contractor basis. Often this work was done during evening hours and on the weekend.

The shearing process for which the company contracted included actual shearing, inspection and nail clipping, if required, and stamping. The practice by the student, however, varied; at times he would carry out all three operations, at others, bargaining unit employees would perform the stamping.

During 1963 the union orally protested the stamping of sheep by the student, and the company allegedly represented that the student needed the money and would be graduating at the conclusion of the 1963 season in any event. The union, therefore, permitted such a practice without further protest in 1963.

In June of 1964 the company employed an outside contractor for two days to carry out the shearing operation. This shearer employed a number of members of his family, and they worked as a group in order to complete the shearing within the two-day period. During 1964, the outside contractor carried out all three processes: shearing, inspection, and stamping.

The union grieved that the above arrangement violated Article XIII of the master agreement between the parties. Unable to resolve the grievance, the parties submitted the following issue to the arbitrator:

> Did the Company violate Article XIII of the Master Agreement by having the sheep stamped by the sheep shearer, an outside contractor, instead of assigning the work to bargaining unit personnel during the month of June 1964?

APPLICABLE CONTRACT PROVISIONS

Article XIII—Subcontracting

The Company will not contract out work to individuals or
to other companies which is normally performed by bargaining unit employees when the necessary equipment is
at hand, qualified employees are available, project completion dates can be met, and the results would otherwise
be consistent with efficient and economic operations.

POSITION OF THE UNION

The stamping of sheep has been performed by bargaining unit
employees as a routine and day-by-day activity for a long period of
time. Bargaining unit employees have carried out the stamping on
newly born animals and on a semiannual basis when the identification
marks have become faded through weathering. This activity was
carried out exclusively by bargaining unit employees at all times
other than during shearing.

The work of stamping is a fundamental part of the process of
identification. The manner by which it is done at the time of
shearing does not change the duty and function carried out throughout the year by bargaining unit employees using the same equipment.
On the contrary the job of stamping is foreign to the normal process
of sheep shearing as evidenced by the fact that commercial shearers
do not have stencilling equipment. The mere fact that the company
has given outside contractors the responsibility and pay to carry out
the stamping work and the mere fact that the company has told
shearers to stamp certainly do not give the company the right to
make such an assignment. The bargaining unit employees in question have no specific job but perform a multitude of operations including the care, handling, and identification of animals. Clearly,
stamping is a part of the operation of identification of animals.

In 1963 the union protested against the stamping activity being
carried out by the outside contractor. The company at the time replied that 1963 was the last year that the college student would be
shearing, an implication that the stamping would no longer be carried out by the shearer. The company was also persuasive in its
point that the student needed the money. At no time during this pro-

test did the company raise the issue that it had the right to make
such an assignment.

The company's action deprived bargaining unit employees of
overtime work which they would otherwise have enjoyed. Therefore,
they should be given monetary relief in the amount of thirty-two hours
of pay, the amount of liquidated damages to which the parties have
previously agreed, if a violation is found.

POSITION OF THE COMPANY

Under Article XIII "work normally performed" does not mean
work which could be performed by bargaining unit employees. The
mere fact that bargaining unit employees stamp sheep at times other
than shearing time and the mere fact that they have the skill to do it
do not mean that the stamping of sheep following shearing is work
normally performed by the bargaining unit. Even if it be conceded
that there were instances where bargaining unit employees stamped
the sheep at shearing, it does not follow that this was work normally performed by the bargaining unit. Normal does not mean the
same thing as occasional.

Similarly, the fact that bargaining unit employees may have
violated instructions and stamped sheep which should have been
stamped by the shearer under his contractual arrangement with
the company does not establish that this was work normally performed by bargaining unit employees. Bargaining unit employees
were never instructed to stamp sheep at shearing, and the contractual arrangement with the shearer provided that he would re-
place the stamped number which was removed in the shearing process.

The obvious purpose of Article XIII is to prevent the company
from diminishing the bargaining unit by unnecessarily taking work
normally performed by them and having it done by outside contractors. The clause was not intended to provide for expanding the
bargaining unit by requiring the company to assign work to the bargaining unit which it had not formerly performed. It is important
to note that the size of the bargaining unit has not been affected by
having the outside contractor stamp the sheep at the same time he
sheared them. In fact in the instance in question two bargaining
unit employees were employed on the Sunday in question at double-
time rates in order to assist the shearer in his work.

Union witnesses testified that the union had always complained about the stamping of sheep by the shearer. Yet these witnesses also testified that bargaining unit employees were normally performing the work prior to 1964. These statements are obviously inconsistent. If they were normally performing the work, there was no reason for them to complain each year that the shearer was stamping the sheep. The fact that the union protested the stamping of sheep in 1963 and the company indicated that the existing arrangement would soon be discontinued, since the student would graduate, does not amount to an admission that the stamping of sheep under these circumstances was work which rightfully belonged to the bargaining unit.

Under the circumstances, the stamping of sheep becomes an integral part of the shearing process. The shearer grasps the sheep and shears it, clipping the nails as required. At the conclusion of shearing, the shearer still has the sheep in his grip. Under these circumstances the only sensible way to stamp the sheep is to have the shearer do it. The convenience and efficiency of doing it in this manner accounts for the fact that the shearer was asked to do this as part of the contractual arrangement.

Suggested Discussion Questions

(a) In interpreting Article XIII the union urges that the interpretation of the term "work normally performed" be considered in the broad framework of the function, for example, in terms of the function of identification, which was regularly performed by bargaining unit employees, rather than in terms of the specific tasks which these employees carried out. What evidence might the union submit to advance such an interpretation, and what evidence might the company submit to combat it? What other factors might be noted by the arbitrator in interpreting the terms in question?

(b) The company denies that at any time it instructed its own employees to carry out the stamping operation during the shearing process, but on the contrary that it designated this as a task to be performed by the outside contractor. What responsibility, if any, does the company have to make certain its instructions were carried out? Would failure of the company to assume its

above responsibility give rise to any adverse consequences in
your decision? Explain.

(c) The company makes much of the inconsistency between the
union's continued protest over not being awarded the disputed
work and its later claim that it was work regularly performed
by bargaining unit employees in the past. Was there any inconsistency in the company's handling of the problem?

38. The Roger Company Case

BACKGROUND OF THE CASE

In March of 1965 the company, a steel fabricator, entered into
a contract with a local junk dealer to dismantle and remove two
machines from the plant. During the same month the company contracted with a local transfer and hauling company to move eight
machines from the third floor of one plant building to the second
floor of another plant building.

In April of 1965 the company entered into a contract with a local
welding firm to weld and to repair wire basket cargo containers.

The union grieved the above actions of the company as a violation
of a well-established practice and working condition under which dismantling, removal, and transfer of machinery has been performed
by bargaining unit millwrights and welding and repair of cargo containers has been performed by bargaining unit welders. Upon denial
of the grievance, the union filed a demand for arbitration.

APPLICABLE CONTRACT PROVISIONS

Section 2—Scope of the Agreement

B. Local Working Conditions

The term "local working conditions" as used herein
means specific practices or customs which reflect
detailed application of the subject matter within the
scope of wages, hours of work, or other conditions
of employment and includes local agreements, written

or oral, on such matters. It is recognized that it is
impracticable to set forth in this Agreement all of
these working conditions, which are of a local nature
only, or to state specifically in this Agreement which
of these matters should be changed or eliminated.
The following provisions provide general principles
and procedures which explain the status of these matters and furnish necessary guideposts for the parties
hereto and the Board.

* * *

3. Should there by any local working conditions in
   effect which provide benefits that are in excess
   of or in addition to the benefits established by this
   Agreement, they shall remain in effect for the term
   of this Agreement, except as they are changed or
   eliminated by mutual agreement or in accordance
   with Paragraph 4 below.

4. The Company shall have the right to change or
   eliminate any local working condition if, as the
   result of action taken by Management under Section
   3—Management, the basis for the existence of the
   local working condition is changed or eliminated,
   thereby making it unnecessary to continue such
   local working condition; provided, however, that
   when such a change or elimination is made by the
   Company any affected employee shall have recourse to the grievance procedure and arbitration,
   if necessary, to have the Company justify its action.

* * *

Section 3—Management

The Company retains the exclusive rights to manage
the business and plants and to direct the working forces.
The Company, in the exercise of its rights, shall observe
the provisions of the Agreement.

The rights to manage the business and plants and to
direct the working forces include the right to hire, suspend, or discharge for proper cause, or transfer, and

the right to relieve employees from duty because of lack
of work or for other legitimate reasons.

POSITION OF THE UNION

The work of dismantling machinery and of removing it to an
area of easy access for pickup by draymen is normally done by
millwrights. The union cites some five specific incidents to support
its position. Likewise the transfer of machinery from one plant area
to another is work normally carried out by millwrights. The union
cites some eighteen specific incidents where millwrights had engaged in transfer activities and ten additional incidents where they
had set up machinery for production operation. These incidents
cover a period of more than twenty years. Indeed, the method for
moving the machines from one floor to another by means of a trap
door was originally conceived and developed by the millwrights.

The millwright crew cannot be considered fully employed at the
time of the incidents in question since one employee was on sick
leave, one on layoff status, and others had bumped into other jobs
within the plant. Thus, the company could have recalled the millwright on layoff and replaced the sick employee with another millwright who was at the time in question employed on other work with
the company. The company could also have used spare shop laborers,
as was the former practice, to help transport machines.

The welding of cargo containers needing repairs had always been
carried out by bargaining unit welders. Although the welders were
currently employed on other projects at the time of the company
action, a member of the bargaining unit working elsewhere in the
plant had previously bid into this group. The company refused to
allow him to perform this work, stating he did not have the requisite
skill. The union urges, however, that the employee in question
should have been given the opportunity to learn the welding skills
involved by having other welders teach him on the job.

In each of the above instances of contracting out, the company
has not followed a well-established past practice and, therefore, is
in violation of Section 2(B) of the agreement. A prohibition against
subcontracting need not be specifically contained in the agreement,
however, since arbitrators have frequently imposed an implied limitation on contracting out where a past practice of performing given
work within the bargaining unit has existed. The union requests that

the employees affected by the company action be awarded retroactive compensation.

POSITION OF THE COMPANY

The union has failed to prove the existence of any agreement,
either oral or written, which limits the right of the company to subcontract work to outside contractors. The projects in question occur
at such infrequent intervals that they cannot be considered under or
included with conditions falling within the provisions of Section 2(B)
of the agreement. It then follows that "past practice" or "local
working conditions" cannot be the issue. Rather the issue is the
company's right to decide when and what type work can be subcontracted without challenge from the union.

The company admits that the union is correct in its facts when
it cited numerous instances where similar work was performed by
bargaining unit employees. It cites, however, a substantial, if not
identical, number of occasions where similar work to that in question
has been contracted out.

All of the company's work force that could perform such work
were actively employed in the plant on the projects in question or on
other essential duties at the time subcontractors were engaged for
this work. The company urges that the subcontracting in question
was of a temporary nature and had no permanent impact on the scope
of the bargaining unit. It did not result in the layoff of any bargaining unit employees. It did not result in the reduction of work
opportunity for the work force employed by the company at the time
of the incidents in question since all of its available working force
with requisite ability was actively employed.

Selected Discussion Questions

(a) Section 2(B) of the agreement cited above has been the target
of considerable labor-management discussion, particularly
during the negotiations immediately prior to the 1959 steel
strike. Interpretation of this provision raises the question of
not only what is a "past practice" but also what is a "practice"
coming under the specific protection of this provision. Is there
a distinction? Explain.

(b) In the light of your answer to question (a) on the preceding
     page, do you believe that subcontracting of the type in question
     in the instant case is protected under Section 2(B) of the agree-
     ment ?

(c) Both parties in the instant case submitted a number of other
     arbitrators' opinions on the issue. Do you think that the
     opinions of other arbitrators are more relevant or less rele-
     vant in this type of issue ?

(d) What specific factors prevailing in the instant case were criti-
     cal in helping you reach the decision which you reached ?

Bibliography

Crawford, Donald, "The Arbitration of Disputes Over Subcontracting, "
    Challenges to Arbitration, Proceedings of the Thirteenth Annual
    Meeting, National Academy of Arbitrators, Washington, D. C.,
    January 27-29, 1960 (Washington, D. C.: Bureau of National
    Affairs, 1955), pp. 51-77.

Dash, G. A., Jr., "The Arbitration of Subcontracting Disputes, "
    Industrial and Labor Relations Review, January, 1963, pp.
    208-220.

Greenbaum, M. L., "The Arbitration of Subcontracting Disputes:
    An Addendum, " Industrial and Labor Relations Review, January,
    1963, pp. 221-234.

Joseph, M. L., "Protect Your Freedom to Subcontract, " Harvard
    Business Review, January-February, 1963, pp. 98-102.

Stone, Morris, Managerial Freedom and Job Security (New York:
    Harper & Row, Publishers, 1964), chap. ii, "Subcontracting:
    The Implications of Silence, " pp. 22-49; chap. iii, "Subcon-
    tracting: Negotiated Restrictions, " pp. 50-66.

CHAPTER 10

The Impact of Technological Change

One of the basic problems of a dynamic society is to achieve two goals simultaneously: first, to operate efficiently its productive resources; and, secondly, to protect its work force from the insecurities brought about by increasing efforts for greater efficiency. From the vantage point of the arbitrator, however, the macrocosmic problem seems overshadowed by the microcosmic conflict of management and unions over the respective needs of the former to innovate, to improve, or even to maintain its competitive efficiency and the legitimate interests of the latter in preserving the job security of employees.

The arbitrator may find the agreement of much less help in resolving issues of technological change than in resolving other contract issues. Few agreements define the term technological change, and many agreements make no specific reference to the treatment of employees affected by its impact. The arguments of the respective parties, therefore, are frequently couched in the language of management's reserved rights and its implied obligations. This is of little help to the arbitrator who must grapple with the problem of what rights management has given up in the contract and what obligations it has assumed, albeit by implication, when faced with problems of employee disruption resulting from technological change. Nor can past practice provide any reliable guide to the interpretation of ambiguous agreement language, for in most cases the entire economic setting out of which the practice arose has been subject to considerable modification. Thus, the thoughtful arbitrator must seek some accommodation between the agreement and the problem which has been created, between contract provisions and the realities of the situation, and between general procedures and special needs. Frequently he develops his own criteria in the process.

What, for instance, does a technological change imply? Is it limited to the mechanization of manual work and the replacement of the man by the machine? Or does it also include those organizational changes initiated by management which integrate and modify job duties, unaccompanied by any mechanical aids?

The impact of these changes fall most frequently in the area of changed work loads and changed work assignments. The mere fact that management has the right to determine work loads does not answer the question of whether a given work load represents a reasonable assignment. Rather the arbitrator must determine this as a matter of fact, rather than rely on contract language or a theory of inherent management rights.

Changed work assignments bring into play all sorts of complex issues. They disrupt previously agreed-upon seniority schedules, upset agreed-upon wage schedules, and introduce jurisdictional issues between members of the bargaining unit who are in different seniority districts and issues between bargaining unit and nonbargaining unit personnel.

When technological changes result in substantial changes in the composition of jobs, what standards should the arbitrator develop to aid him in setting a proper wage rate? Frequently the new job cannot be adequately described or classified under the parties' agreed-upon methods for rate classification. Should the arbitrator attempt to warp the essential characteristics of this job into an outmoded and somewhat irrelevant classification system, yet one that bears the authentication of the parties, or does he have an extra contractual responsibility to develop different, but more relevant criteria?

When the result is the creation of jobs of substantially different character, what criteria can be formulated for determining whether they are properly considered bargaining unit or nonbargaining unit jobs? Should a standard be established entirely through an historical study into the elements of these jobs as they have been performed in the past? Should the inherent nature of the present duties be controlling? Should the inherent capacity of contending bargaining unit employees to perform the newly structured jobs be considered? Should the impact on the bargaining unit be a factor?

These same questions arise when separate seniority groups of bargaining unit employees are contending for opportunity to perform the newly created job. An additional problem is created here for the union cannot avoid favoring one group of its members over another. This may serve to cripple the presentation of its evidence, and the arbitrator must guard against receiving too partial a presentation of the facts, or against receiving too little information on which to base a reasoned decision.

CASES

39. The Linden Company Case

BACKGROUND OF THE CASE

One of the products manufactured at the Trenton, New Jersey plant of the company is linoleum. Among the processes used by the company in the manufacture of linoleum is that of bleaching and sealexing which is carried out by a series of operations incorporated into the bleaching and sealexing line. On January 28, 1963 after prior notification to the union on January 24, 1963, the company reduced the crew size on the bleaching and sealexing line by eliminating the job classification, "roll supply and utility," and redistributing the duties previously performed by the two employees holding that classification among other crew members, namely the rollmaker, rollmaker helper, reliefman No. 1, and reliefman No. 2. These changes were made effective on the processing of light and standard gauge linoleum (household weight) but not on heavy gauge linoleum (commercial weight).

The essential work involved in the above job changes concerns the transporting of linoleum rolls (jumbo rolls) from storage to the jack-in station of the bleaching and sealexing line and from the jack-out station of the line to storage, as well as assisting in introducing new rolls into the line at the jack-in station and assisting in removing rolls processed by the line at the jack-out station. Jacking-in and jacking-out are terms which characterize the splicing of a new roll of material to the previous roll undergoing the process and the unsplicing of the already completed roll at the conclusion of the process.

The impetus for the company's action in changing the crew size resulted from several factors: first, increasing utilization of the bleaching process; secondly, introduction of improvements in the equipment; and, thirdly, greater managerial control over the length of the roll.

The bleaching process was introduced into the line in 1959. During the past three years the proportion of household linoleum receiving bleach increased from 45 per cent to approximately 80 per cent. When bleach is not applied, the roll speed through the line (at times other than roll changes) is approximately 190-200 ft. per minute; where bleach is applied the roll speed drops to some 75-85 ft. per minute. Thus, with a greater proportion of the product undergoing bleach, the roll speeds have dropped significantly, with a consequent reduction in the number of jack-ins and jack-outs required per shift.

During the years 1960-1961 a number of improvements were made in the equipment used in performing the operations of transportation and storage of rolls, as well as that used in jacking-in and jacking-out. In summary, these changes reduced the time and effort required to carry out the operations, decreased the number of operations per shift through the use of larger rolls, and increased the time span during which the jacking-in and jacking-out procedures could take place without the necessity of stopping the process.

Greater managerial control over the length of the jumbo roll has reduced the number of incidents wherein jacking-in and jacking-out would occur simultaneously. The length of the sheet of material within the line is 1,000 feet; thus, with rolls of approximately 1,000 ft. in length, the jacking-in and jacking-out would occur almost simultaneously. By avoiding these critical lengths, the need for simultaneous jack-ins and jack-outs has been reduced. Since each jack-in and jack-out procedure takes approximately a minute and one-half, should these operations be required simultaneously there is still some flexibility for their performance within a time span short enough to avoid a stopping of the line by reducing the speed of the line to some twenty-five feet per minute and feeding the line and/or storage roll from the festoons each of which stores 150 feet of material. Should this prove insufficient, the line can be stopped, although this creates some product damage.

Industrial engineering studies inaugurated in 1961 and continued in 1962 indicated to the company that considerable idle time existed in the jobs of rollmaker and rollmaker helper, as well as in the classifications at issue, roll supply and utility. As a result of these detailed studies, scrap handling duties were removed from the job of the two reliefmen and assigned to another bargaining unit classification, scrapman, and the classification of roll supply and utility was eliminated, the duties of that classification having been redistributed to the jobs of rollmaker, rollmaker helper, and the two reliefmen.

Following the elimination of the classification of roll supply and utility, the occupants of that classification, Messrs. George Marx and Robert Burnham, were assigned to other classifications at no reduction in rate.

The union grieved the action of the company on March 10, 1963, as follows:

> Union objects to the Company reducing the crew size on the Bleaching & Sealing and waxing operation which is in violation of the Collective Bargaining agreement.

Upon denial of this grievance by the company, the union filed a demand for arbitration.

APPLICABLE CONTRACT PROVISIONS

Article VII—Wages

(A) A schedule setting forth hiring rates, base rates, and job rates will be contained in and made a part of each local Supplemental Agreement.

* * *

3. There appears on Exhibit A the job rate payable for each job. As to any changes thereafter, the COMPANY will notify the LOCAL UNION promptly after the date of change.

4. The COMPANY shall establish rates for all new or altered operations after ten days, but not later than thirty days from the start of such operations. The LOCAL UNION shall be notified promptly of the establishment of such rate. Any protest by the LOCAL UNION, with respect to such rate, must be initiated in writing, within thirty days after receipt of notification, and shall then be subject to the Grievance Procedure provided in Article V of the Master Labor Agreement. Any adjustment made shall be retroactive to the date

of the start of the new operation or date of
change in job content.

5. It is recognized that the COMPANY has the responsibility for setting up new or altered operations which affect job content. The COMPANY
will inform and discuss new or altered operations
in advance, with the LOCAL UNION Officers, with
regard to the extent and nature of the changes.
Prior to establishing rates for altered operations,
employees will be given opportunity to review the
job analysis for their job.

POSITION OF THE UNION

The company possesses only those rights expressly granted by
the agreement, and the agreement confers no right to abolish a job
and/or classification. Indeed, Article VII of the agreement obviously limits the company to the right of altering an operation.
But altering an operation is quite different from eliminating or
abolishing an operation. In the instant case, no technological
changes were made and the operation was not altered. The flow of
work is precisely the same as before the reduction in crew size
took effect; each element is unchanged. All that is altered is the
identity of persons performing the duties of men eliminated from the
crew.

Article VII of the agreement freezes both the job classifications
and the wage rates paid thereto for the life of the agreement. While
the company may alter jobs, it may not eliminate or abolish classifications listed in the wage section of the agreement.

The company did not exercise good faith in the manner in which
it handled the crew reduction. In April, 1962 the company was well
aware of what it wanted to do; its studies were completed. At that
time the parties were in negotiations. Instead of putting this issue
squarely on the bargaining table where it properly belonged, the
company waited some nine months after negotiations were concluded
and then abruptly announced its decision to the union and put the plan
into effect with but four days' notice.

The company should be directed to recreate the classification
of roll supply and utility and assign to this operation the two men
who by seniority are entitled to the job.

POSITION OF THE COMPANY

The company has the right, in good faith, to eliminate, to add, or to reassign work and thus to eliminate, to create, or to change jobs during the term of a collective bargaining agreement unless that right has been restricted in the agreement. Not only does the present agreement contain nothing to restrict the company's rights in this regard, but on the contrary Article VII expressly recognizes this right. Control of the work structure is a fundamental and essential function of the management of a company. Following this principle, the mere listing of classifications and the rates paid thereto in the agreement does not freeze jobs for the length of the agreement.

The argument of the union that job changes may be made if there are modifications in equipment is an unreasonably narrow view which finds no support in the agreement. Nothing in the agreement expresses a distinction between various types of reasons for job changes. There may be a change in materials, a change in process, or a change in technique, any of which may require job changes fully as much as a change in machinery. Logic and reason dictate that the company be in a position to take advantage of all improvements so that they may be passed on to the consumer in improved or less costly products.

In any event in the instant case substantial equipment changes had the effect of reducing the time and effort required to perform the duties of the job in question. The company points to the new hoists and rails, the other equipment for handling larger rolls, and the increase in the capacity of the festoons. That these changes were made over a period of time and that the effect of these changes was cumulative should not affect the issue, particularly when as here, there were other significant developments. The increase in the proportion of linoleum being bleached with a consequent reduction in the speed of the line was equally significant in reducing work at the jack-in and jack-out positions. The development of the technique of jumbo roll size control was the key that cleared the way for the job changes.

The company has made job changes in the past under prior contracts with provisions identical to those in the instant agreement, and in none of the prior instances was there a challenge by the union to the company's right to do so. These prior job changes confirm completely the express and apparent meaning of Article VII to the effect that the company has the right to change, eliminate, and create jobs during the term of the agreement.

The changes were made in good faith for sound business reasons. The crew of the bleaching and sealexing line was studied thoroughly using sound and proper industrial engineering techniques. Studies were also conducted after the changes to assure beyond all question that the changes were reasonable. Even after the changes, the studies showed that the rollmaker was working no more than 70.9 per cent of the work day and the rollmaker helper no more than 77.7 per cent of the work day, not including paid lunch and break time of fifty minutes per day, and not including short idle periods.

The union did not challenge the accuracy of the company's studies. It had the opportunity, if it wished, to have its own time study engineer study the jobs and testify, but it chose not to do so. Nor did it, as it easily could have done, produce any employee who worked on the line who was able to refute the company's findings. There were no complaints from employees, as individuals, that they were carrying an unreasonable burden or that there was the slightest difficulty in the working of the bleaching and sealexing line according to the uncontradicted testimony of company witnesses. The company's findings, therefore, must be accepted as accurate.

Suggested Discussion Questions

(a) To what extent, if at all, does the listing of job classifications in the agreement restrict the company's right to alter jobs? Explain. Do you think the company's position might be strengthened by a management clause? Explain.

(b) What were the company's responsibilities with respect to this matter during the negotiations of 1962?

(c) In support of its position the company supplied the arbitrator with some twenty-six detailed exhibits of various industrial engineering studies. The union argued that the arbitrator should not admit such studies as evidence since the company did not discuss these studies in advance with the union as required by the provisions of Article VII, A, (5). How would you treat such evidence? Explain.

(d) Suppose you found that the company did not fully carry out its

responsibility to discuss the new changes with the union, although the company had the right to make the crew change.
What remedy might be provided "to make the parties whole"?

40. The Fletcher Company Case

BACKGROUND OF THE CASE

The company manufactures felt-based linoleum. The operation
in question is that of adding color to the surface of the linoleum
through the use of giant flatbed printing machines which are approximately one hundred feet in length. The grievance concerns the No. 1
Print Machine.

The linoleum is introduced into the No. 1 Print Machine inter-
mittently in eighteen-inch lengths. During the interval from one
feed to the next, a series of printing blocks extending the full width
of the linoleum descend to the linoleum surface and apply a portion
of color to the linoleum. The linoleum then proceeds through the
press for a further eighteen inches where another similar series of
printing blocks in like manner apply a different portion of the color.
This process continues for the length of the press until the multi-
colored pattern is completed.

The blocks in turn receive an application of paint for transmittal
to the linoleum while they are in a raised position. This is accomplished by means of the carriage, a circulating roller which is partly
immersed in a tray of paint and which in rotation brushes the bottom
surfaces of the printing blocks.

The paint used on the No. 1 Print Machine is mixed in the paint
mixing department. After it is received in the print department, the
color pourer on the crew of the No. 1 Print Machine conditions the
paint, that is, thins it to the proper consistency for the above-cited
operation.

Prior to November 19, 1964 paint was supplied to the carriage
trays by the use of hand pails. Occasionally it was necessary to
stop the machine in order to permit the color pourer to spread the
paint evenly through the carriage trays. As of the above date, the
company installed an automatic conveyor system which conveyed
paint from the paint tubs directly into the carriage trays. One re-

sult of this change was a substantial reduction in the paint required for application; the amount of paint applied under the new system was reduced from .50 pounds per square yard to .28 pounds per square yard. Thus, only approximately half as much paint had to be conditioned. The new equipment also automatically spread the paint evenly along the carriage trays. On the above date the company also installed a clock and lost-time meter on the cut-off (back) end of the No. 1 Print Machine. These devices recorded the time lost as a result of stoppages of that machine and reduced the work load of the checkers.

During 1963 the industrial engineering department of the company had conducted a work load study of each employee in the print department. The union had been advised of such a study and invited to conduct a study of its own, if it so desired, but it did not do so. The results of this study for the eleven man crew of the No. 1 Print Machine were as follows:

Title	Per Cent of Time Worked	Per Cent of Available Time	Per Cent of Available Time After Relief of Other Employees and Allowable Personal Time
Machine Runner	39	61	50
Second Hand	32	68	57.3
Color Pourer #1	27	73	60.3
Color Pourer #2	47	53	54.8
Color Pourer #3	44	56	45.5
Rack Man #1	41	59	46.8
Rack Man #2	67	33	20.8
Checker No. 1	38	62	49.5
Checker No. 2	46	54	43.3
Helper	68	32	19.4
Roll Man	22	78	65.6

Based on the technological improvements made on the No. 1 Print Machine as well as on the study of work loads made the previous year, the company announced on November 15, 1964 to both the crew of the machine and to their union stewards that it was reducing the crew size to nine men by the elimination from the crew of one color pourer and one checker. On November 16, 1964 the company met with the grievance committee and explained the reasons for the company's action.

On November 19, 1964 the union filed the following grievance:

Department Grievance is hereby started on Monday,
November 19, 1964 concerning action taken by the Company
in the elimination of one Color Pourer and one Checker
from the crew of the #1 Print Machine, because of the
installation of flexible hoses and pumps, and of the installation of a clock and a lost-time meter on the cut-off end
of that Print Machine.

We, the men of the crew of the #1 Print Machine,
claim that the work is still there for the two men that the
Company intends to take off that Print Machine on each
shift, and we do not agree with this move. This move
will add more work on the Machine Runner, Second Hand,
Color Pourer, Rack Man, Checker, Helper, and Roll Man
since they operate as a crew.

To which grievance the company submitted the following answer:

These changes occurred after and as a result of the
installation of new equipment, relocation of equipment,
and revision of procedures and techniques. These involved more than the equipment changes mentioned in the
written grievance. Industrial engineering studies have
confirmed that the job changes were justified and desirable.

At the Third Step of the Grievance procedure, the
Union position was that the Company violated Paragraph
33 in addition to Paragraph 2 of the current Agreement.
There has been no violation of these provisions nor of any
other provisions of the Agreement. As a matter of fact,
possibility of job changes is expressly recognized in the
Agreement.

Unable to resolve the dispute to its satisfaction, the union filed a
demand for arbitration.

APPLICABLE CONTRACT PROVISIONS

Paragraph 2

The COMPANY and the UNION specifically waive any
rights which either may have to bargain with the other
during the term of the Agreement or any extension thereof

on all matters pertinent to rates of pay, wages, hours, and other terms and conditions of employment, and the parties intend this Agreement, during the term hereof, shall constitute final settlement of all negotiable matters between the UNION and the COMPANY.

Paragraph 6

The UNION agrees that its members will individually and collectively perform loyal and efficient work and service and will use their influence and best efforts to protect the property of the COMPANY and the COMPANY'S interests, and will assist in promoting the sale of the COMPANY'S products, and that they will cooperate with the COMPANY and the employees of all departments in promoting and advancing the welfare of the COMPANY and its sales at all times. The COMPANY agrees that it will cooperate with the UNION in its efforts for harmony and efficiency among the COMPANY'S employees.

Paragraph 15

(a) A list of jobs and corresponding rate for each job is supplied by the COMPANY to the UNION herewith and made a part of this Agreement.

(b) Rates on new jobs or altered jobs shall be the subject of bargaining between the COMPANY and the UNION. Start of such bargaining shall begin not later than forty-five days after date on which any such job is filled except as may be otherwise mutually agreed between the COMPANY and the UNION.

Paragraph 33

There shall be continued in effect any current plant practices or working conditions which supplement but do not conflict with any provisions of this Agreement and which fall in such nonproductive categories as smoking privileges, relief for personal needs, off-the-job lunch periods, and the like.

POSITION OF THE COMPANY

For many years the company experimented with equipment which would satisfactorily eliminate the hand filling of carriage trays. It finally succeeded in solving this problem. As a consequence there is little work to be performed by the color pourer once the pumps have been started. Moreover, the reduction in the amount of paint used under the new method is greatly reduced, thus reducing the amount of time required to be spent by the color pourer in conditioning paint. The company points out that the material saving in this factor alone amounts to almost $30,000 per annum.

The action of the company was also justified by the results of the prior work load study taken under the old method. This study clearly indicated that even before the technological changes, No. 1 Print Machine was being inefficiently operated on the basis of an eleven man crew. One color pourer was working only 27 per cent of the available time and one checker only 38 per cent of the available time. With the introduction of the technological changes on the machine, color pourers and checkers, as well as the crew as a whole, would be working at even lower percentages of the available time.

These work load studies were taken with the full knowledge of the union and the employees undergoing the study. More than 2,960 readings were taken and analyzed. Of the work elements observed, 80 per cent were judged as being performed at normal pace, 4 per cent were judged as slow, 16 per cent were judged as too fast a pace. This indicates the fairness of the rating procedure. Adequate fatigue and personal time factors were allowed. Professor Grant, a recognized authority in the field of industrial engineering, testified that the procedures were sound and the conclusions reached were valid. Despite the opportunity offered it by the company, the union did not make its own studies. More important, it did not challenge the validity of the company studies. Further studies taken in February and March of 1965 by the industrial engineering department indicated that each member of the crew of No. 1 Print Machine had substantial available time, although color pourers and checkers had less available time than they had enjoyed previously.

None of the eliminated employees was laid off, but all were transferred to other jobs paying equivalent or higher job rates. Subsequently, when production schedules were reduced, there were layoffs of a few employees whose jobs had been taken by displaced color pourers and checkers.

Absent clear and compelling contract language to the contrary, employers have the right to change work procedures and job duties. No such contrary contract language has been evidenced in the instant situation.

POSITION OF THE UNION

The action of the company effectively reduced the pay of five of the six employees who were eliminated from the crew of No. 1 Print Machine. Their elimination from that machine also caused six other employees to be downgraded. The standard wage rates set forth in the current agreement cannot be changed during the life of the agreement. Moreover, the duties and responsibilities of color pourers and checkers have been unilaterally changed by the company during the term of the agreement. Such action violates Paragraphs 15(a) and 33 of the agreement. Any such changes must be negotiated. Paragraph 2 of the agreement completely closes all negotiable matters until negotiations for the next succeeding contract are under way. Thus, print department wage rates and conditions of employment are completely barred from negotiation during the life of the existing agreement.

Since the company has by unilateral action violated the terms of the collective bargaining agreement, the arbitrator should direct the company to reinstate a color pourer and checker to each of the three shifts and to pay those who have been eliminated from those jobs the difference in pay between those jobs and the jobs in which they have been working.

Suggested Discussion Questions

(a) Should the arbitrator admit as evidence work load studies taken by the company after the date of the grievance? Explain carefully indicating to what extent and for what purpose evidence collected after the date of the grievance is admissible.

(b) The union position is essentially based on tying Paragraphs 15(a), 33, and 2 of the agreement together. Do you believe such an interpretation is valid in the instant situation? Explain in the light of the principle of contract construction that the contract must be interpreted as a whole.

(c) The company position seems based on the argument that such changes in crew complement could have been made in the absence of technological changes based on the inefficient utilization of manpower under the former method. Do you agree? Explain.

(d) The company argues that the impact of the technological change had no adverse consequences on the eliminated crew members. To what extent, if at all, is a determination of this question essential to the resolution of the overall issue?

41. The Haddon Chemical Company Case

BACKGROUND OF THE CASE

The company is engaged in chemical operations. Its main product groups are phenol, carbohydrates, phthalics, and napthalene. Its operations are characterized by continued product and process obsolescence which has been accompanied by drastic changes in the job content of employees.

The instant grievance concerns the operations of the maintenance department. Prior to 1962 this department was organized on a "craft shop" basis, composed of such units as the pipe, machine, and electrical shops. Each shop was headed by a foreman (and in some instances an assistant foreman in addition) and had its own office, but the personnel of each shop serviced equipment throughout the entire plant on a craft basis. Although maintenance personnel from a given craft frequently worked in conjunction with personnel of other crafts, supervision was carried out on a strict craft basis. The bargaining unit classifications assigned to each shop were mechanic leader, mechanic—first class, and helper.

The instant grievance is concerned with the work assigned to the mechanic leader. Prior to 1962 the mechanic leader in each shop performed the following general categories of work:

(a) Obtained work to be performed by their shop. Maintenance work was initiated by operating supervisors usually on written "Request for Maintenance Work" forms, but sometimes requests were first made orally to a particular shop foreman's office. There was no hard rule as to whom these requests had to be made, and they were given to shop foreman, mechanic leaders, and even to mechanics. Work requests specified the location of work, description of work, the craft shop involved or principally involved, and whether the work was an emergency or not. There was normally a backlog of these work requests in the various shops awaiting completion.

(b) Estimated whether jobs requested cost more or less than $50. Work in excess of $50 in cost had to be approved by the maintenance supervisor's office and a special identifying number (red card number) was issued. This estimating was performed by both maintenance and operating supervisors as well as the mechanic leader. More often than not the mechanic leader did the estimating of over or under $50, although the company alleges he was insufficiently trained to estimate in more precise amounts. Moreover, the company alleges that when the mechanic leader requested a red card number for work over $50, he was allegedly questioned as to the particulars of the job by the maintenance supervisor.

(c) Eliminated job hazards. Mechanic leaders were required to report safety hazards to the company and take steps to eliminate them. They also filled out, in part, forms called "work and flame" permits which were a combination order to complete the job and a safety checklist. These forms had to be signed by operating foremen before a job was started and after its completion. The forms were also filled out by foremen and mechanics as well as mechanic leaders.

(d) Filled out time cards. Mechanic leaders filled out "job time cards" accounting for the total man-hours spent on a particular job. These forms were also filled out by foremen and mechanics.

(e) Assigned and reassigned men to jobs. Normally on
Monday mornings company supervision designated a
maintenance crew to work with a mechanic leader for
the week, although these assignments were subject to
change daily. The foremen specified priority jobs.
Usually the mechanic leader assigned his men to particular jobs, and usually the mechanic leader reassigned
them upon completion of specific jobs. Sometimes,
however, supervision made both original assignments
and reassignments to the crew.

(f) Obtained mechanics from other shops for jobs. Where
a job required the work of two or more crafts, co-
ordination of personnel was required. Sometimes
this was done by the foreman of the "master craft"
(the one having the major portion of the work), sometimes by the operating supervisor working through the
respective mechanic leaders.

(g) Authorized men to obtain materials. Parts were obtained upon requisitions signed by foremen. At times,
however, foremen issued signed requisitions in blank
which were filled in by mechanic leaders in the field
who gave them to mechanics who obtained the parts
from the storeroom or small parts depot.

(h) Supervised one or more gangs of men in their work.
Since shop personnel worked alone or in small groups
throughout the entire plant, they were often widely
scattered at considerable distance from the foreman's
office. When in the field, men were subject to supervision by mechanic leaders, and mechanic leaders
were responsible for the work the men performed and
their conduct, although foremen also frequently supervised the men. Mechanic leaders did not have authority to discipline.

(i) Worked with tools in varying degrees, although the
proportion of time varied, and the amount of manual
work to be performed was left to the discretion of
each shop foreman.

(j) Supervised shutdown work. Major maintenance pro-

jects involved shutting down equipment, and this usually occurred at night. Mechanic leaders took regular
turns at these assignments and did many of the afore-
said tasks (usually to a greater degree owing to the
absence of the normal complement of supervision)
under the overall supervision of foremen.

(k) Within the category of other, general duties, instructed
less experienced mechanics and read blueprints.

In June of 1962 a new maintenance system was instituted in the
West Oil Area. Essentially this system was one of planning and
scheduling all maintenance jobs and of supervising the work performed on an area rather than a craft basis. An area staff was
formed composed of a foreman, assistant foreman, coordinator,
and estimator. The essentials of the new system were as follows:

A new job request form was instituted which, though similar
to the form previously in use, incorporated a detailed estimating
table and a work and flame permit. This form was completely
filled out by operating and area maintenance supervision. These
forms were assembled by the coordinator for scheduling.

After operating supervision was consulted for priority information, daily planning sessions between the area foreman, coordinator, and the respective shop foremen were held to plan a
daily schedule of work for the following day. This schedule was
supplied to the respective shop foremen and to operating supervision.
Parts requisitions were also prepared by the area foreman, and
scheduled deliveries were made to the work area by storeroom employees prior to initiation of given jobs. The new system also included control features.

This system has affected the aforementioned duties of the
mechanic leader in the following ways:

(a) Mechanic leaders no longer obtain work from operating supervisors, but from their own foremen.

(b) Mechanic leaders no longer estimate whether jobs
cost over or under $50.

(c) Mechanic leaders no longer fill out work and flame
permits as authorization to start work.

(d) Mechanic leaders no longer fill out job time cards.

(e) Mechanic leaders no longer assign or reassign men to jobs.

(f) Mechanic leaders no longer obtain mechanics from other shops for jobs.

(g) Mechanic leaders no longer authorize men to get materials.

(h) Mechanic leaders no longer supervise one or more gangs of men in their work.

(i) Mechanic leaders now work with tools substantially full time.

(j) Mechanic leaders still essentially supervise shutdown work since it is usually done at night and the new system is only operative Monday through Friday, 8 A.M. to 4:30 P.M. At night and on weekend work the mechanic leaders' duties are essentially unchanged.

(k) Mechanic leaders still instruct less experienced men and read blueprints.

No change has occurred in the number of mechanic leaders employed and no change in their job classification or rate of pay.

The union grieved the action of the company and, unable to resolve the dispute earlier in the grievance procedure, the union filed the following demand for arbitration:

What disposition shall be made of the "Mechanic Leader" grievance?

The Union requests the Arbitrator to direct the Company to discontinue assigning the work of the "Mechanic Leader" to people outside the OCAW bargaining unit.

POSITION OF THE UNION

The duties of the mechanic leader were transferred to two new job classifications outside the bargaining unit, namely those of co-ordinator and estimator respectively. These classifications had never been used previously to perform this work and represent classifications which had not previously contained these responsibilities.

Such unilateral action violates the recognition clause, since under the agreement the union is recognized as the exclusive bargaining agent concerning the wages, hours, and working conditions of the mechanic leader. Yet the union was not consulted over the transfer of the duties of the mechanic leader.

The action of the company also amounts to a circumvention of its obligation under the seniority provisions of the agreement. By establishing two nonbargaining unit jobs, the company, in effect, grants superseniority rights to employees on those jobs. If its action is upheld, it would be able to lay off mechanic leaders while retaining employees as estimators and coordinators, even though the latter employees would be performing the work of mechanic leader.

The action of the company also violates the wage schedule of the agreement. The classification of mechanic leader was made part of the agreement at a fixed wage rate for the life of the agreement. Whenever the company removes duties and responsibilities from a job, it decreases the value of the job in proportion to the amount of duties removed. If the company can reduce the value of jobs by transferring the duties of those jobs, then the wage and classification structure of the agreement has no meaning.

Such action represents a unilateral change in past practices. The duties of this job had remained constant for over 20 years. Further, the policy of not transferring work customarily performed by bargaining unit employees to nonbargaining unit personnel was established in a prior arbitration award. To uphold the company would in effect destroy the effectiveness of the prior award.

The reorganization and transfer of the work of mechanic leader was not occasioned by economic necessity or loss of business volume which made necessary the elimination of supervision over mechanics. Rather the work that was transferred is being done today as heretofore. The union requests, therefore, that the company be directed to return the supervisory work as heretofore performed by the mechanic leader to that job classification.

POSITION OF THE COMPANY

The duties in question were eliminated rather than transferred. The mechanic leaders served as assistants for foremen with respect

to the nonmechanical functions of this job, the only functions that are
in dispute. These functions were performed by the mechanic leader
because of the inefficient central craft shop organization. When the
maintenance organization was changed to an area basis with compre-
hensive planning and scheduling of all maintenance work, not only
did shop foremen no longer need the mechanic leader to assist them,
but most of the functions of the mechanic leader were either eliminated entirely or placed in a different form in the hand of area supervisors.

The following functions were completely eliminated: estimating
whether jobs cost over or under $50, since now this is calculated on
an exact dollar basis, a function the mechanic leader had never
carried out; obtaining "red cards"; filling out job time cards; and
authorizing mechanics to get materials, since materials are now
furnished by other bargaining unit employees.

The functions of obtaining work, assigning and reassigning men
to jobs, filling out work and flame permits, and coordinating the
personnel of several shops were eliminated as separate unrelated
functions and integrated as a whole in the new method of scheduling
and planning as done by area personnel. Supervision without authority has been eliminated. Area foremen who now supervise men
on the job do so with authority.

Nothing in the agreement expressly prohibits the company from
transferring duties performed by bargaining unit employees to employees not in the bargaining unit. Indeed, the union's construction
of the agreement is contrary to past practice, as evidenced by the
following incidents:

1. In 1958 the union grieved that the company by not replacing a mechanic leader with a bargaining unit employee during a vacation period had, in effect, transferred the functions of a mechanic leader to a nonbargaining unit foreman. The union later withdrew the
grievance.

2. In the 1950s the company created five new assistant
foreman jobs, thus substantially increasing the number
of personnel who performed functions now claimed to
belong to the bargaining unit. One mechanic leader in
this case performed more manual work after the reorganization, but the action was not protested by the
union.

3. In 1954, four operating leaders, whose functions were
   similar to those of the mechanic leader, were promoted
   from their bargaining unit jobs to foremen and thereafter performed the same functions they performed as
   leaders, except that they then had authority to enforce
   their directives. The leader jobs they vacated were
   not filled. No grievance was filed by the union.

4. In another instance, the mechanic leader in the boilermaker shop became ill and was assigned to light duties
   although his rate and classification were maintained by
   the company. The union urged that his old post be filled,
   but the company refused claiming that the foreman could
   get along without the services of a leader because the
   boilermaker shop had been combined with the iron-
   worker shop. The job was never thereafter filled.

These past practices are clearly consistent with the company's
position that it has the right to reorganize and transfer functions.

Neither the recognition clause, nor the seniority provisions,
nor the wage schedule prohibit a transfer of work duties in the instant situation. While some arbitrators have construed recognition
clauses as delineating certain work as belonging to the bargaining
unit, most of these decisions have involved situations where the transfer was not for sound economic reasons, where the work involved
was not clearly supervisory in nature, and where the transfer constituted a substantial part of the work of the bargaining unit. In the
instant situation the reorganization was dictated by sound economic
considerations, was clearly supervisory, and did not result in a
reduction of bargaining unit jobs, but rather allowed bargaining unit
personnel to concentrate more on nonsupervisory aspects of the job.

The seniority provisions provide rights only as between two or
more bargaining unit employees, and cannot be relied on to prohibit
transfers of the nature evidenced in the instant situation. At most,
the wage schedule provides that if an employee performs a certain
job, he will be paid a certain rate.

The union's opposition to the necessary reorganization of the
maintenance department is not to advocate job security, but job
stagnation. True job security can only come when the company
meets or betters competition. The reorganization was necessary
to that end.

Suggested Discussion Questions

(a) The evidence makes clear that some of the disputed work was eliminated, some of it transferred to nonbargaining unit personnel. Do you think the company's right to eliminate work is a more unlimited right under the typical collective bargaining agreement than its right to transfer work? Explain carefully, showing any contractual basis for your reasoning.

(b) In the above case the transfer was to nonbargaining personnel. Do you think the company's rights to transfer work to nonbargaining unit employees are more or less restricted than its rights to transfer work to other bargaining unit personnel? Explain.

(c) The union stresses in its arguments that new nonbargaining unit classifications were created to which the work in question was transferred. Of what importance is this factor as compared to transfer to old nonbargaining unit classifications? Explain.

(d) What criteria would you develop to aid you in your resolution of whether the work transferred constituted a proper or improper transfer? Apply your criteria to the duties in question.

42. The Hammonton Company Case

BACKGROUND OF THE CASE

In September, 1964 the company purchased and installed in its Walnut Ridge plant an automatic external O.D. cylindrical grinder manufactured in Japan and identified as an Okuma grinder. The basic improvement in this grinder is that it automatically shuts off after completing its operation and will automatically switch from rough grind to fine grind at any preset diameter.

The company trained a number of men in the classification of machinist—general A (specialties), labor grade four, in the use of the Okuma grinder. Prior to the advent of the Okuma, these men operated only one grinder at any one time.

In late September or early October the company experimented with the feasibility of having the Okuma operator leave this machine during its automatic cycling and operate a second grinder. On the basis of these tests, a decision was made to commence two-machine operation on a regular basis. At the time which this operation commenced, the second machine was located twenty to thirty feet from the Okuma. This distance, plus concern over possible Okuma malfunctioning, caused certain employees to raise the question of their responsibility for machine damage, material damage, or wheel breakage if it occurred on the Okuma while they were setting up or running the second machine. The employees were informed that they would not be held responsible for these kinds of damage unless it was the result of improper setup on the Okuma.

On October 22, 1964 the following grievance was filed:

> The union alleges that the company is violating the labor agreement by assigning two machines to a single operator other than those which are part of the current agreement and which were negotiated or accepted by the parties.
>
> Such present assignments have not been negotiated with the union and in the absence of a negotiated settlement, the terms and conditions of the labor agreement are binding without change for the duration of the agreement.
>
> Further, the union alleges the company is in violation of Sec. 1 par. 1, Sec. 3 par. 1, Sec. 4 par. 1 and 3, Sec. 8, par. 6.
>
> We ask that a single operator be assigned each machine (except as otherwise provided in earlier labor agreements) until such time as the parties have agreed upon any variation of the existing and current agreement.

Unable to resolve this grievance to its satisfaction, the union filed a demand for arbitration.

Since the date of the grievance, layout changes have been made facilitating two-machine operation, and with the stabilization of the layout arrangement a job evaluation procedure under Section 4, Paragraph 2 of the agreement has been initiated.

APPLICABLE CONTRACT PROVISIONS

Section 1—Intent and Purpose

Par. 1—It is the intent and purpose of the parties

hereto that this Agreement shall insure cooperative industrial and economic relations between the Company and the Union, and shall set forth the basic agreements covering rates of pay, hours of work, and the conditions of employment to be observed between the parties hereto.

Par. 2—It is the intent and purpose of both the Company and the Union to secure and sustain maximum productivity per employee during the term of this Agreement. Both parties recognize the importance in the savings of materials, tools, machinery, and the protection of all Company property.

Section 3—Management

Par. 1—The management and control of the Company and the direction of the working forces, including the right to plan, direct, control, and schedule Company operations, methods of production and processing, the kind and operation of machinery and equipment, the installation of production standards as practiced prior to the date of this Agreement, the right to hire, suspend, maintain discipline, discharge for proper cause, promote, demote, transfer, lay off, and the right to introduce or improve production facilities are vested exclusively in the Company, subject to the provisions of this Agreement.

Par. 2—The Union agrees that it will not oppose or interfere with the efforts of the Company to maintain or improve the skill, efficiency, ability, and production of the working forces, the quality of its products, and the methods and facilities of production, subject to the provisions of this Agreement.

Section 4—Wages

Par. 2—The existing rates on individual jobs in effect at the time of the signing of this Agreement are hereby mutually agreed to for the duration of this Agreement. In the event a new job is added or an existing job is changed to the extent that it requires greater skill and effort to a measurable degree and/or moved into a different labor grade, the procedure to be used in establishing the rate for the job will be as follows: (Following this the Agreement provides for a detailed procedure for the Union to challenge any rate set on new jobs by the Company).

Par. 3—An employee temporarily assigned to work on a job other than his regular job because of lack of work on his regular job, breakdowns, or emergencies, will continue to receive his regular rate of pay for all hours so worked. No temporary assignments under this Paragraph will be made which will require an employee to work on a job in a higher classification than his existing job. . . .

Section 10—Safety and Health

Par. 1—The Company agrees to make reasonable provisions for the safety and health of its employees during the hours of their employment. . . .

POSITION OF THE UNION

Under Section 1, Paragraph 1 of the agreement, the rates of pay and job duties which govern such rates must remain unchanged during the life of the agreement. Requiring the Norton machine operator to operate the Okuma machine simultaneously is a change in conditions of employment which is barred by the above provision.

The management clause (Section 3, Paragraph 1 of the agreement) limits the company in its right to install production standards to those only "as practiced prior to the date of the agreement." The intent of this language is to prohibit the doubling up of jobs. The effect of the company's action is to impose a new production standard beyond that practiced by an operator when he ran only one machine, as he did prior to the date of the agreement. Under these circumstances, the doubling up of jobs went beyond the power reserved to the company under the management clause.

Section 4, Paragraph 3 of the agreement contemplates that each employee shall be assigned to a "regular job." The Norton machine operator's "regular job" was the operation of the Norton machine. When he was required to run the Okuma machine as well, he was clearly performing an assignment beyond that of his regular job. Because of the increased responsibilities and production requirements attached to the new assignment, it was an assignment to a higher classification than his existing job, an assignment therefore barred by the specific language of the above-cited provision.

Though under the provisions of Section 4, Paragraph 2 the company may add a new job or change an existing job, the company may not combine a new job with an old job. In short, such a provision does not allow for job combination.

Even though feasible, none of the jobs on the cylindrical grinder have ever been combined in the past so as to require the operator to perform the simultaneous operation of two machines. When other jobs have been combined in the past the company has negotiated such a combination with the union.

Although the company attempts to rely on Section 4 of the agreement, it should be noted that the company has not established a new rate for the job in question, but has continued the Norton machine rate for the simultaneous operation of the Norton and Okuma machines. Thus, it would appear that the company agrees that the combining of jobs does not result in a new or changed job, but rather asserts that such combinations is an exercise of its right of unilateral action. No provision of the agreement supports this point of view, and indeed such unilateral action without good faith collective bargaining with the union would constitute an unfair labor practice.

The effect of the company's action reduces the need for employees and encourages the spread of unemployment, a result at variance with our national labor policy. Such action, if permitted, will place each existing job in jeopardy and cause an instability in the negotiated work loads and rate structure established in the agreement. In addition, the operator is exposed to increased hazards in the operation of the two machines which adversely affect the health and safety of employees. Employees are forced to do twice as much work for the same pay, a factor which will surely lead to "heightened tensions" on the job. Thus, the cause of equity should force the upholding of the union claim.

POSITION OF THE COMPANY

The right to require employees to perform simultaneous grinding operations on two grinders is clearly reserved to the company under the agreement. The company has historically expressed its concern and need for improvement and efficiency, as evidenced in Section 1, Paragraph 2 and Section 3, Paragraph 2 of the agreement. Further, in Section 3, Paragraph 1 of the agreement, the company has specifically reserved its right to control the operations and methods of

production and the kind and operation of machinery and equipment.
Finally, Section 4, Paragraph 2 of the agreement provides the
mechanism by which job changes can be equated to employee earnings.
By clear implication, such changes in duties are expected to occur.

The union was unable to show that a safety hazard was created
by reason of the combination of machine operations. Testimony of
union witnesses did not support any conclusion that the changed assignment created, in itself, a safety hazard. The company as a
practical matter cannot pledge hazard-free work environment. Indeed, the present rating sheet for job evaluation purposes gives
recognition and job factor points for the possibility of such hazards
as "flying chips, wheel fragments, or work pieces," "the possibility of hand or foot injury in handling parts," and "cuts or eye injuries due to chips or turnings, and burns from torch brazing equipment." All of these potential injuries are common hazards associated with machine tool operation and the addition of the Okuma
grinder did not materially alter their existence.

The reference to production standards in the management clause
of the agreement does not prevent the company from combining jobs
or adding job duties. Testimony on the meaning of this language
was at best inconclusive. Company witness Lever stated that the
language referred to time standards. Union witness Ambler stated
that the intended meaning was broader than time standards, but admitted that the union had never specifically related the language to
job combination during any negotiations. The specific language falls
far short of being a clear and express limitation upon the company's
right to change job duties during the life of the contract. Moreover,
assigning such a meaning is inconsistent with the clear language of
Section 4, Paragraph 2 of the agreement which specifically provides
for job changes. The union argues that the combination of jobs differs from the addition of job duties. This is a distinction without a
difference. It also assumes, quite incorrectly, that operation of the
Okuma grinder was at some time a separate and distinct classification which the company now sought to combine with other grinding
operations.

Contrary to the union picture, no evidence was introduced which
tended to show any inclination by the company to destroy either the
union or the employee's job security. Instead, the evidence indicated that the company is adjusting and modernizing in an orderly
fashion to meet competition. The union can scarcely profit from

a freezing of job duties to the extent that such a freezing imperils the company's competitive position and jeopardizes the job security of all. The instant change in job duties has not resulted in any loss of jobs, but rather three additional employees have been added to this job classification. The new arrangement increased competitive efficiency without any increase in scrap or damage. It is managerially sound and in the best interests of all concerned.

Suggested Discussion Questions

(a) Both the union and the company commented upon the question of whether the simultaneous operation of two grinders created an increased safety risk. To what extent, if any, should this influence the arbitrator in his decision?

(b) Since the parties cannot agree on their intent in incorporating the words "production standard" in the agreement, what guides are available for the arbitrator in interpreting this language? Do these guides support the union or management position in this case?

(c) Evaluate the relevance of Section 3 of the agreement as applied to the facts of the instant case.

(d) Would a decision for the company be clear permission for the company to combine other jobs in the plant? Explain carefully. How might the union achieve increased protection in this regard?

43. The Berlin Company Case

BACKGROUND OF THE CASE

On April 7, 1964, the company communicated to the union its plans for replacing an existing chain conveyor with an employee-driven monorail conveyor for the movement of transports of yarn and empty bobbins between the extrusion and textile departments of the company. The relevant parts of this communication are, as follows:

In accordance with the provisions of Paragraph 8 of our
Collective Bargaining Agreement, we are notifying you
now of a significant change which will be made in our
yarn conveying equipment and operations starting on or
after May 8, 1964.

Basically, this change involves the removal of the existing chain conveyor between Extrusion and Textile Departments and a substitution of a mobile, individually
operated conveyor suspended from an overhead track.
This will improve both employee efficiency and our capacity to move transports of yarn to important areas within
the two buildings.

To varying degrees, the work now performed by the following classifications will be affected by this change:

> Twisting Servicemen
> Bobbin Stores Male
> Coning Servicemen
> Coning Exam Servicemen
> Beaming Servicemen
> Bobbin Stores Female (Yarn Exam)

Basically the essential elements of the work of servicemen under
the old system were to push or to tow transports filled with bobbins
of yarn or empty bobbins to and from the various textile operations
(spinning, bobbin stores, twisting, and so forth) and to and from the
various fixed stations at which these transports could be connected
to the overhead conveyor for interdepartmental moves. Each of
these servicemen was responsible for intradepartmental moves
within his particular department or area which moves were manually
handled, and he was also responsible for loading and unloading the
transports from the overhead conveyor which carried the transports
between departments.

One key aspect of the job was in learning the identification system composed of a coding key on the various bobbins so that yarn
of the proper size and composition would be delivered to the proper
machines, and that delivery could be made to the conveyor in accordance with the schedule from which the serviceman worked.

Twisting department servicemen also serviced supply buggies,
picked up waste yarn, segregated beaming yarn, and carried out

other minor operations. Servicemen were not completely eliminated under the new system.

Under the new system a conveyor operator is employed in
driving or operating an overhead monorail conveyor. Small cabs
on both ends of the conveyor contain the controls. Since the conveyor is designed to get much closer to the various textile machinery, manual moves have been greatly reduced. The conveyor
operator stops the conveyor where transports are waiting, usually
at the ends of aisles, loads them on the conveyor by manually pushing
them into position under the conveyor and actuating a mechanical
hook arrangement, and delivers them in accordance with his schedule throughout the various departments serviced by the conveyor.

After numerous discussions between the company and the union,
the conveyor operator job was initially staffed on November 1, 1964.
On December 3, 1964 the union filed the following demand for arbitration:

> The Union protests rate for "Conveyor Operator." Relief
> Sought—The Union requests that in accordance with the
> terms of Article XV of the Agreement that the rate for
> this job should be $2.33 per hour retroactive to the date
> of the establishment of this job.

As the time of the filing of the demand, the rate for the job in
question was fixed at $2.08 per hour. A subsequent general wage
increase brought this to $2.16 per hour. In the arbitration hearing
the union asked that the demand be amended to show that the relief
sought was for $2.41 per hour in order to maintain the 25-cent in-
crease originally sought.

APPLICABLE CONTRACT PROVISIONS

Paragraph 8—Cooperation

(c) In order to attain more effective employee performance and efficiency, consistent with safety, good
health, and sustained effort, the Employer shall have the
right to change existing working assignments or to establish new working assignments. The Employer will notify the Union in writing of such changes.

(d) The Union agrees to cooperate with the Employer
in securing employees' acceptance of the new or changed

working assignments and will earnestly endeavor to secure the performance of the duties assigned to the employees.

(e) The Employer will notify the Union in writing
thirty (30) days prior to the effective date of such change
and furnish detailed information pertaining thereto, including time-study data if the result of time studies is
the basis on which the new or changed work assignment
is to be established.

(f) Reasonable effort shall be made to reconcile
differences before the installation of changed or new
work assignments. If agreement is not reached, the
Employer may proceed to install the work assignment.
If thirty (30) days after the new or changed work assignment has been instituted by the Employer, the Union is
still dissatisfied, the matter may be referred to arbitration. In the event the Union decides to arbitrate the
work assignment, the case must be filed with the Arbitration Association within sixty (60) days from the effective date of the assignment, unless extended by mutual
agreement.

Paragraph 15—Rates for New Jobs

(a) If, during the term of this Agreement, a new
occupation is established or if there is a change in method
or process in an existing occupation, the new or changed
occupation will be rated by the Employer and the Union
notified in writing of such rating prior to the effective date
of the rating.

(b) The Employer and the Union shall promptly discuss the proposed rating in an effort to reach agreement.
Should the parties fail to agree on the proposed rate, then
the Employer shall have the right to establish and apply
the proposed rate for a trial period of one month. If, at
the end of the trial period, there is a disagreement as to
rate, this will constitute a grievance to be appealed through
the Grievance and Arbitration procedure. Failure on the
part of the Union to file for arbitration within sixty (60) days
from the effective date of the Company's proposed rate shall
constitute acceptance on the part of the Union of the Company's proposed rate.

(c) If the rate is changed as a result of a joint review with the Union or as a result of arbitration, the changed rate will be retroactive to the date when the occupation was established or changed.

(d) At the request of the Union an officer of the Union shall be allowed access to the Plant to study the new or changed occupation in any case where there is a dispute over the rate.

Schedule A					Hourly Pay Rate Schedule				
Job Classification	Start Rate	1st Mo.	2nd Mo.	3rd Mo.	4th Mo.	5th Mo.	6th Mo.	7th Mo.	8th Mo.
Machinist	$2.45	—	$2.53	—	$2.58	—	$2.75	—	—
Mechanical servicemen	1.94	—	2.02	—	2.15	—	2.25	$2.41	$2.60
Case strapper	1.76	$1.82	2.05	$2.18	2.33	—	—	—	—
Label machine operator	1.76	1.82	2.05	2.18	2.33	—	—	—	—
Shipping checker	1.82	1.87	1.94	2.08	2.29	—	—	—	—
Floor buffer	1.77	1.83	1.97	2.11	2.26	—	—	—	—
Loaders, yarn	1.81	1.86	1.93	2.07	2.23	—	—	—	—
Case marker	1.73	1.80	1.86	2.00	2.23	—	—	—	—
Beamer	1.76	1.82	1.90	2.03	2.22	—	—	—	—
Coner	1.76	1.82	1.90	2.03	2.22	—	—	—	—
Twister	1.76	1.82	1.90	2.03	2.22	—	—	—	—
Vacuum cleaner operator	1.76	1.86	1.94	2.00	2.19	—	—	—	—
Textile servicemen	1.75	1.80	1.86	2.00	2.16	—	—	—	—
Coal handlers	1.67	1.73	1.78	1.87	—	—	—	—	—

POSITION OF THE UNION

A comparison of the job of conveyor operator with the former duties of the various servicemen with respect to the skill required, the responsibility exercised, and the work effort involved indicates that the rate of the conveyor operator should be increased. The key factor of the job according to the company is the skill or knowledge required in the identification of bobbins. The company admits that there has been an increased number of identifications which the conveyor operator must recognize as compared to the former serviceman. With the increase in the speed of the conveyor, 180 feet per minute as against forty feet per minute of the old conveyor, obviously the conveyor operator must carry out this identification function, the more skilled function, a greater percentage of his working time. The identification function has, therefore, become a larger proportion of his job. Although the distance which a transport is manually moved has been significantly decreased, the increased number of transports handled and the increasing frequency with which they are moved by the conveyor operator indicates that the physical effort of tugging, pulling, and positioning expended by the conveyor operator is at least equal to that expended formerly by the serviceman, if not greater than the former level of exertion. The conveyor operator exercises increased responsibility with respect to his own safety, damage to company equipment, and the safety of others. He must be careful to keep his head, hands, and feet inside the cab during movement. He could now damage twelve transports against the one or two he was manually moving. He could possibly damage more by running the conveyor into transports parked along the alleyway in which it moves. The danger of running over other employees is much greater in the new operation than in the former manual operation.

The company has removed the most skilled duty of the various servicemen, that of identification, and transferred it to the conveyor operator, yet it has retained the rate of $2.08 (now $2.16) per hour for that job for those servicemen who have been retained. If the rate of $2.08 is proper for existing servicemen, who now do the lower-skilled portions of the job, and the union agrees that it is, then it is inequitable to pay the conveyor operator that same rate. The conveyor operator should be paid more than the servicemen considering the respective duties each carries out at the present time.

An increase of twenty-five cents per hour would not destroy the relationship of existing rates. A rate of $2.41 per hour would place this job between the advanced skills of the mechanical craft group and the jobs of female operators (beamers, coners, twisters) who are still performing work of lesser responsibility in a more confined area. The job should certainly be placed between the higher evaluated jobs of the mechanical group and the vacuum cleaner operator or the floor cleaner or buffer operator. An increase of twenty-five cents per hour should, therefore, be directed for the job of conveyor operator retroactive to the date of its establishment.

POSITION OF THE COMPANY

The company has no formal job evaluation system but rates are negotiated. A management group which knew all of the details of the respective jobs considered the rate question and found the conveyor operator's job "not in excess" of the serviceman's requirements. Consideration was given to effort, and it was determined that the conveyor operator's job was less arduous and involved less gross work. It generated less tensions than the serviceman's job since it is evenly paced by the speed of the monorail unit. The job was a preferred job in the plant; all of the servicemen desired it since it carried the status factor of riding around in a cab. While the monorail conveyor moves relatively rapidly, the speeds are preset and the conveyor operator simply starts and stops the unit. Switching arrangements within the cab are not complicated controls, but relatively simple. The operation of the monorail unit is simple and requires only the appropriate skill of an automobile driver. Although the job requires considerable mental alertness, so does the job of serviceman. The most important element of both jobs is the proper identification of yarns, which was slightly increased with respect to the conveyor operator. The responsibility of both involves selecting the proper yarn at the proper place and delivering it to the proper place. Although damage to equipment is possible in the conveyorized transport, damage to equipment and machinery is also possible in the manual moving of transports.

The company considered the elements of effort, skill, and responsibility, and also the balance of the proposed rate with the general wage structure. It knew all the rates and all the jobs. While the union listed various rates in the plant, the contents of these jobs were not in evidence, and no valid comparisons can be made among them. The company did not fix the rate lightly or capriciously but upon mature reflection and consideration of all proper factors. The union should not, therefore, on the showing made in this case ask the arbitrator to substitute his judgment for that of the company in setting the rate for the conveyor operator's job.

Suggested Discussion Questions

(a) Although the company concedes that the identification skill of the conveyor operator is greater than that required of the

serviceman and requires some additional training, it contends
that the rate currently paid the serviceman is sufficiently high
to reward the additional skill required of the conveyor operator.
Evaluate this argument in the light of the parties' methods for
determining rates of pay.

(b) With respect to the identification skill requirement, the union
contends that the conveyor operator spends a higher proportion
of his time on this more highly skilled component of his job and,
therefore, is deserving of a wage increase. Evaluate this argument.

(c) The company maintains that the mechanically paced operation
carried out by the conveyor operator creates less tension on
the job and requires less mental alterness than the operation
did formerly when it was carried out by the serviceman when
the pace of the job was totally within the control of the employee
himself. How would you evaluate this argument?

(d) The company implicitly argues that the arbitrator should not
substitute his judgment for that of the company in the absence
of arbitrary, capricious, and discriminatory action. Is this
a more valid argument in the case of setting rates for changed
jobs than it is in disciplinary matters? Explain.

(e) Suppose as the arbitrator you were convinced that the job in
question deserved some rate increase. How would you go about
determining the proper amount of the increase? Are any guides
available? Explain.

Bibliography

Chamberlain, Neil W., "Job Security, Management Rights, and
Arbitration," Labor Arbitration—Perspectives and Problems,
Proceedings of the Seventeenth Annual Meeting, National
Academy of Arbitrators, New York City, January 29-31, 1964
(Washington, D. C.: Bureau of National Affairs, 1964), pp.
224-240.

Kennedy, Thomas, "Merging Seniority Lists," Labor Arbitration
and Industrial Change, Proceedings of the Sixteenth Annual

Meeting, National Academy of Arbitrators, Chicago, Ill.,
January 23-25, 1963 (Washington, D. C.: Bureau of National
Affairs, 1963), pp. 1-44.

Seward, Ralph T., "Reexamining Traditional Concepts," Labor
Arbitration—Perspectives and Problems, Proceedings of the
Seventh Annual Meeting, National Academy of Arbitrators,
New York City, January 29-31, 1964 (Washington, D. C.:
Bureau of National Affairs, 1964), pp. 240-251.

Stone, Morris, Managerial Freedom and Job Security (New York:
Harper & Row, Publishers, 1964), chap. viii, "Attrition and
Automation," pp. 204-238.

Index

Aaron, Benjamin, 23
Accident record (*see* Discipline)
American Arbitration Association, 3
Arbitrability:
  in general, 7-23
  procedural irregularities, 8-9
Arbitration:
  hearings, 4
  procedures, 3-4
Arbitrator:
  authority, 5-6, 7-23
  contrasted to judge, 4-5
  function, 4-8
  permanent vs. *ad hoc,* 3
  selection, 3
  sole vs. board of arbitration, 3
Assignment of work (*see* Work assignments)

Bailer, L. H., 116-117
Bargaining history, 58-62, 74-77, 141-144
Belcher, David W., 70
Bernstein, Irving, 70
Bibliography:
  arbitrability, 23
  discipline, 45-46
  overtime distribution, 167
  seniority, 144-145
  subcontracting, 182
  technological change, 219-220
  vacation and holidays, 90

Bibliography (Cont.)
  wages, 70
  work assignments, 116-117
Bonus payments (*see* Wages)

Chamberlain, N. W., 219
Christmas bonus, 58-62
Crawford, Donald, 182
Crew size, reduction in, 92-93

Dash, G. Allan, 23, 182
Davey, H. W., 45
Davis, Pearce, 70, 117
de minimis violations, 112-116
Discipline:
  accident record, 26-29
  constructive discipline, 38-41
  denial of contract benefits, 157-160
  due process, 25
  entrapment, 25
  extenuating circumstances, 25
  fights and altercations, 29-32
  horseplay, 38-41
  in general, 24-46
  indirect discipline, 157-160
  insubordination, 33-38, 42-45
  just cause, 24
  propriety of penalties, 25
  refusal to work, 42-45
  statute of limitations, 41

Disputes:
  over interpretation of contract, 2
  over new contract terms, 2
Due process (*see* Discipline)
Dunlop, John T., 70, 90

Establishment of new shift, 99-104

Fairweather, O., 117
Federal Mediation and Conciliation
  Service, 3
Fights and altercations (*see* Discipline)
Fleming, R. W., 23
Fringe payments (*see* Wages)

Greenbaum, M. L., 182
Grievances:
  policy grievances, 8, 10-14, 66
  time limits on filing, 8

Healy, James J., 70, 90, 144
Holiday pay:
  eligibility, 71-72
  eligibility for:
    laid off employee, 81-82
    on leave of absence, 77-81
    right of annuitant, 74-77
    surrounding day requirement, 72,
      77-81, 81-82
  fringe benefit provisions, 71-72
  monetary loss provisions, 71-72
Horlacher, J. P., 144
Horseplay (*see* Discipline)
Howard, Wayne E., 144-145

Initial Contract, 58-62
Insubordination (*see* Discipline)

Job classifications:
  changes in job content, 48
  effect on work assignments, 94-99,
    105-108, 108-112
  evaluation of jobs, 50-54
  fractionating job classifications, 94-
    99
  and technological change, 184, 186-
    192, 206-212, 212-219

Joseph, M. L., 182
Just cause (*see* Discipline)
Justin, Jules J., 23, 70

Kennedy, Thomas, 219

Livernash, E. Robert, 70, 90
Living document theory, 2, 19

Medical testimony, value of, 126-129

Negotiation history (*see* Bargaining
  history)

Overtime distribution:
  absentee employee, 148-150
  definition of overtime work, 164-
    167
  deliberate bypass of employee, 160-
    164
  emergency work, 148-150
  failure to post schedules, 148-150
  failure to report, 157-160
  in general, 146-167
  overtime vs. fill-in work, 150-154
  practice as a factor, 157-160
  remedies for violation, 147, 155-
    157, 160-164
  technical violation, 160-164
  temporary transfer of employees,
    150-154

Plaut, Frank, 23
Privileged conversation, 45, 104

Refusal to bargain, 54-58
Refusal to work (*see* Discipline)
Rubin, M. L., 117

Sayles, Leonard R., 145
Schmertz, Herbert, 23
Seniority rights:
  ability limitation on exercise, 119-
    120, 121-126, 133-136, 137-141

Seniority rights (Cont.)
  in general, 118-145
  in lateral transfers, 141-144
  in layoff, 119, 121-126, 130-133, 133-136
  in promotion, 119, 137-141
  nature of service, 119, 121-126
  physical fitness limitation, 120, 126-129
  problems in application, 118-120
  trial periods, 130-133
  unit for application, 119, 133-136
Seward, Ralph T., 220
Slichter, Sumner H., 70, 90
stare decisis, principle of, 4
Statute of limitations (*see* Discipline)
Steelworker trilogy, 7
Stessin, L., 45
Stone, Morris, 23, 45, 90, 117, 145, 167, 182, 220
Subcontracting:
  criteria for judging propriety, 169
  during layoff, 170-173
  express provisions, 169, 173-178
  in general, 168-182
  past practice as guide, 170-173, 178-182
  silent contract, 168-169, 170-173
Sussman, A. M., 45-46

Taylor, George W., 145
Technological change:
  definition, 184, 186-192
  effect on job classification, 184, 186-192, 206-212, 212-219
  effect on other contract provisions, 184
  effects on bargaining unit jobs, 184-185, 198-206
  effects on crew size, 186-192, 192-198
  elimination of duties, 198-206
  implied obligations of management, 183-184
  in general, 183-220
  jurisdictional problems, 185
  past practice as guide, 183-184
  management rights, 183-184, 186-192, 192-198

Technological change (Cont.)
  responsibility to discuss changes, 186-192
  safety considerations, 206-212
Teele, J. W., 46
Transfers (*see* Work Assignments)
Trial periods (*see* Seniority rights)
Trotta, Maurice S., 70, 90

Vacation pay:
  eligibility, 72-73
  eligibility for:
    anniversary date, 82-86
    eligibility date, 82-86
    laid off employees, 82-89
  fringe benefit provisions, 72
  monetary loss provisions, 72
  prorating of, 73
Vacations and holidays, 71-90

Wages:
  bonus and fringe payments, 49, 58-62
  changes in job content, 48
  election day pay, 66-69
  exemption of disputes from arbitration, 47-48
  in general, 47-70
  incentive rates, 48-49, 62-66
  job classification, 50-54
  wage level disputes, 47-48
  wage reopening, 47, 49, 54-58
Wagner Act, 1
Wallen, Saul R., 117
Work assignments:
  de minimis violations, 112-116
  emergency situations, 105-108
  fractionating job classifications, 94-99
  in general, 91-117
  interchange, 92
  effect of job classifications on, 94-99, 105-108, 108-112
  management's rights, 94-99, 99-104, 108-112
  non-bargaining unit employees, 91-92, 112-116
  out of department, 105-108
  permanent changes, 92-93
  temporary transfer, 92